HORROR
and
VIOLENCE
The DEADLY DUO In The MEDIA

Phil Phillips and **Joan Hake Robie**

HORROR and VIOLENCE

The DEADLY DUO In The MEDIA

Phil Phillips and Joan Hake Robie

STARBURST PUBLISHERS™

P.O. Box 4123, Lancaster, Pennsylvania 17604

Phil Phillips, evangelist/author, conducts multi-media seminars on toys, games and cartoons and their effect on children. Phil has appeared on television and radio shows throughout the United States and Canada and has been written about in *USA Today, Newsweek, Dallas Times Herald, The Sun* (Baltimore), and *El Paso Times,* to name a few.

Joan Hake Robie, editor and ghostwriter of best-selling *Turmoil In The Toy Box (1)* (Phil Phillips), is author of ten books, which includes *Halloween And Satanism, Turmoil In The Toy Box II,* and *Horror And Violence—The Deadly Duo In The Media.* Joan has appeared on TV shows such as Geraldo Rivera, Sonja Live in L.A., People Are Talking, and Heritage Today. She has been a regular guest (as a conservative-moral activist) on The Morton Downey Jr. Show. Her radio shows include USA Radio, Christian Broadcasting Network and Moody Network's Open Line. Joan is in demand as a speaker and conducts seminars throughout the country.

To schedule Author appearances write: Author Appearances, Starburst Promotions, P.O. Box 4123, Lancaster, PA 17604 or call (717)-293-0939.

Credits:

Unless otherwise noted, all Scripture quotations are from the King James Version.

Cover Art by Kerne Erickson.
Illustrations by Leslie Walton.
Editorial Assistants: Linda Straitiff and Gale Martin.

We, The Publisher and Authors, declare that to the best of our knowledge all material (quoted or not) contained herein is accurate; and we shall not be held liable for the same.

First Printing, September 1988
Second Printing, November 1990

ISBN: 0-914984-16-0
Library of Congress Catalog Number 88-60884

Printed in the United States of America

Dedication

*To all persons who are concerned about the Horror,
Violence, and Sex that permeates the media—
and to those who are willing to do what is necessary
to stop it!*

Contents

Introduction

How many people did you watch getting murdered, maimed, mugged, or robbed last evening while in the comfort of your living room? Did you enjoy the rapes and shootings that you saw on the screen during your most recent Saturday night out? Did your teenager tell you about the latest "slasher" film that he rented at the local video shop? Did he describe the expression on the face of the half-naked woman as the "sicko" repeatedly stabbed her with a knife, and chopped at her with an axe before he beheaded her then tossed her body parts aside like the day's garbage? If your child rented the video on a Monday or Tuesday, he only had to pay about a dollar for this "wonderful" bit of cinematography. The age of your child is no barrier, due to the fact that the producer released it "not rated."

Do you think these authors are alarmists? No, we are not—the images of horror and violence are stepping off the big and little screen to assault minds and hearts alike, and you are paying for it in ways other than the cable fees, tape rentals, or theater tickets. Sad to say, there are parents, even Christian parents, who are watching and permitting their children to watch violence at a rate like no other generation. You must open your eyes to the problem and take action before it is too late.

We have written this book not only to make you aware of the problem of media horror and violence with eye-opening statistics and research information, but more importantly to share our own advice, as well as that of noted experts, on how to combat the violence that is so severely damaging your family and others across America and around the world.

Phil Phillips and Joan Hake Robie

1

A Visual Banquet
Of Brain Tissue

"SHOOT HIM, SHOOT HIM!" shouted the crowd
of onlookers. "SHOOT HIM. SHOOT HIM AGAIN!"
The account of the story:
A 25-year-old police officer was accosted, without
provocation, by a stranger. While they wrestled, the man
managed to grab the officer's gun and ordered him to
get on his knees and beg for his life. When the policeman
acquiesced to his request, the man turned and started
to walk away. At this point, the crowd which had gathered
to watch the action began to chant, "Shoot him, Shoot
him!" The man turned and shot the police officer three
times in the head while the crowd shouted, "SHOOT HIM
AGAIN!"

Violence is everywhere. Although there may be many
reasons, the question that most often arises is: "Does
watching violent television movies and videos affect our
actions or the actions of our children?" Can you believe
that there are parents who shrug off the fact that their
children are watching violence at a rate like no other
generation? Since 1982 there has been an increase of over
720 percent in violence in children's programming.

Film and video have almost unlimited capability to
capture violence in ways that it rarely, if at all, could be
seen in reality. The use of special effects has advanced
to the point where we can view a man having his head

blown off from only inches away—expanding an event in time that might last one second into "a visual banquet of brain tissue." *Everything from the camera angle to editing and music is used to cultivate and heighten the sensation of fear, horror, and shock.*

We authors, Phillips and Robie say: The subject of violence in the media (television, movies, videos, books, newspapers, magazines, etc.) is very controversial and really hits home in numerous households. In many minds, the lengthy debate over the effects of violence in cartoons, movies, and television upon those who view it will continue to rage, regardless of what these authors say. Violence in the media is irrefutably popular and is the source of enjoyment for many people.

One of our main concerns about violence in the media is that it cultivates an insensitivity to violence in reality. Violence on TV is often depicted casually with little, if any, emotional, physical, or long range consequences to anyone involved in the dramatization. We ask you, "Is the constant exposure to indiscriminate violence in the media turning children into a generation calloused to the pain and suffering of others? Will the children of the 'media age,' who are nourished on a diet of violence, be capable of reacting with compassion and resolve when real violence is being perpetrated, or will they be passive and unable to react to the violence in the real world?"

A Hollywood Producer's Tale

When asking questions about the subject of violence in the media, one always has in the back of his mind the most extreme conclusion concerning those viewing violence: Are we, indeed, programming a generation of mass murderers who axe or shoot their way through their frustrations or problems? Or, is violence in the media simply a reflection of our society as Steven Bocho and many like him assert? Steve Bocho has spent his entire adult life writing and producing at Universal City Television Studios. He made this statement about TV violence: "I believe that entertainment is by and large a reflection of our real world, certainly violence has a place in our popular entertainment." To those in our modern society who would agree with Mr. Bocho we ask, "When was the last time that you witnessed a rape, a murder, or even a car accident?" We believe that popular entertainment is not a reflection of our society, rather it is a driving force to change the reality and social norm of our culture. Here are some startling facts:

Phoney TV

- In an average evening of TV viewing, deadly weapons appear about nine times per hour.
- The average child has watched the violent destruction of more than 13,000 persons on TV by the time he is fifteen.
- Film and video have almost unlimited capability to capture violence in ways that rarely, if at all, could be seen in reality. The use of special effects has advanced to the point that, as was previously mentioned, we can view a man having his head chopped off by an airplane propeller from only inches away, expanding an event in time that might last one second (and would be deadly to the viewer from the position of the camera) into an audio-visual banquet of sight and sound featuring dissentegrating human tissue.
- The typical American child sees on television 75,000 incidents of drinking by the age of 21.[1] The percentage of movies containing the use of alcohol is 89 percent. This brings the consumption of alcohol in movies to at least 1000 percent more than consumed in reality.
- A survey of current movies conducted by the National Coalition on Television Violence (NCTV) revealed that rape occurs in 18 percent of the films. This was equivalent to one in six films.[2]

Turn It Off

"The Father of Electronic Television," Vladimir K. Zworykin, at the age of 84 confessed that his favorite part of the TV is the "off" switch. Many agree, arguing that if violence and other aspects of the media bother you, turn it off, or don't go to see it. Although numerous people besides ourselves get a sense of satisfaction from doing just that, it is more than an oversimplified answer to a complex situation.

Television affects even those who do not watch it. A child who does not watch violence in cartoons or other forms of media will be affected by its presentation if he becomes the subject of violent aggression from one of his peers who has been exposed to a barrage of media violence. A child who is hit over the head by a playmate learns indirectly from imitation of media violence to act violently.

NCTV estimates "25-50 percent of the violence in our society comes from the culture of violence that has been established and gets reinforced every day by violent entertainment."[3] There has been a 300-500 percent (per capita) increase in violence in our society in the course of the past 30 years. This makes NCTV assertions and findings truly alarming.

My Pal, TV

Most children, by the age of two or three, regularly watch 26-30 hours of television programming each week. This translates into the more startling fact that no other generation in the history of mankind since creation has gained a major portion of their "socialization" from a machine. Consider for a moment the cultural values that this machine is teaching the general public.

Sex and Violence on Television

Sex on television was practically nonexistent in the early sixties, unlike today's television. **In soap operas almost everybody is fornicating or committing adultery or even incest. 98 percent of all sexual scenes in "soaps" represent fornication. Nothing is off limits—euthanasia, homosexuality, abortion, drugs, child abuse, alcohol, rape, and murder. Violence is being presented in many forms.**

Is violence only to be considered harmful if it upsets our emotional sense of decency and well being, or is violence shrouded in cultural acceptance to be dealt with?

A person's basic reaction to a segment of violence in a movie can, on the average, be determined by with whom in the movie they identify. In a film that leads the viewer to relate with the victim of the violence being portrayed, there is a tendency to experience repulsion to what is being viewed. However, if the movie leads them to identify with the villain, a negative perception of the violence portrayed will almost *never* occur.

Therefore, **we are telling society that it is okay for the good guy to use violence, however excessive, as long as he beats the bad guy. Some people, we believe, are swayed by "good vs. evil" to the extent that they become tolerant of the means involved.**

Censor The Trash

Whose responsibility is it to censor the trash out of television? Is only violence that is considered to be repulsive for whatever reason to be eliminated, or do we look at the effects of all types of violence on our children, ourselves, and our society to determine what is appropriate for viewing? Are our children to grow up believing that guns are an important part of every day life? Are we, even inadvertently, encouraging children to use aggression as an acceptable means of settling disputes? Can we condone barbarism being peddled as patriotism?

2

We Live In A Violent World

All first time parents get advice on how to take care of newborns. Sometimes this information is passed on from friends, and sometimes through books or classes. Whatever the source, most parents expect that they will need a formula, diapers, bottles and special clothes for their baby. One very important item that is not mentioned on anyone's list could be called "resources to make the baby a human being." *Humanizing* is as large a responsibility as feeding, diapering and cuddling. Though newborns are lovable, precious, and cuddly to their parents, consider all that they have yet to learn about being human beings.

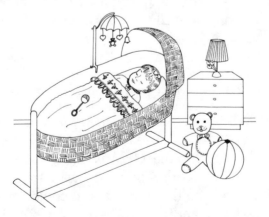

Children must learn to feed themselves, to dress themselves, to talk, to follow rules, to know right from wrong, and to value and believe in things. Newborns are totally unknowing and dependent, waiting to learn many things. The process of learning to be human is commonly called *socialization.*

Through socialization children learn the beliefs, behaviors, and values deemed significant and appropriate by other members of society. Socialization is necessary and beneficial as a way of regulating behavior. As children are taught the ways of their culture and interact with people around them, they develop the skills, attitudes, and knowledge to contribute to their communities. This amazing process teaches children attitudes shared by whole cultures of people. For instance, in ·the Hindu culture, children learn to worship and not eat the cow, while in America children learn that the cow is just another farm animal. Socialization can teach beliefs shared by entire cultures, and still leaves plenty of room for individual personality development.

The Universal Parenting Machine

The Universal Parenting Machine (UPM) was designed to imagine how children might develop without any human contact. The imaginary UPM experiment would be carried out as follows:

> Six babies (three boys and three girls) are placed into a universal parenting machine directly after birth. The UPM is a self-contained building, equipped with all the machinery needed to tend to the babies' physical needs. The machine is constructed so that the babies can survive for the first 18 years of life without any human contact.

The ideal setup for the UPM would be that it would look like our own world, complete with trees, flowers, and a domed roof, so that the children could see the sun, clouds, rain, snow and stars. The UPM would be made as pleasant as possible, lacking only one feature: all other humans beings. Can babies learn to be human without learning from other human beings? Without anyone's example, would the children play with one another? Would they become friends, or feel love toward one another? Would they learn to talk with each other? Would they express thoughts and ideas? Would they naturally cooperate with one another, or would they tend to be aggressive? Would they develop rules within the UPM, and share values as to what is good and what is bad?

There is no information to collect on the results of such an experiment. We can only make educated guesses, based on what we know about how children learn. There are several expert theories on how children learn to become human. In fact, when it comes to how children develop, we are all theorists, so to speak. Most of us can and do suggest why children "turn out the way they do." Some of us believe that a necessary way to control child behavior is the occasional smack on the backside. Many such "mini-theories" exist for use in many specific situations. For right now, we'll look at three very *broad* theories of how children learn that experts use to understand behavior, and to predict future behavior.

How We Learn

Sigmund Freud considered childhood emotional developments to be the "building blocks" of the grown-up personality. Psychoanalysts believe that the methods parents use to raise their children have a very marked effect on their personality development.

Others believe that almost all human behavior is learned, rather than something that we are born with. Support and punishment are the best ways for parents, teachers and others responsible for helping children behave in socially acceptable ways.

Still others believe that children's minds develop through a series of stages. A person's level of intellectual development determines how that person sees the world, and what he will learn from living with other human beings.

What Makes Us Tick

For many years, those who study human development have argued the three opinions concerning human nature:

1. Are children born *good* or *evil?*
2. Can children be molded by parents and others?
3. Is the process of human development completed in *stages?*

Good or Evil?

Is man good or evil from birth? This question has been argued for centuries. The belief in original sin says that children are born as sinful and negative creatures who need molding from parents to be good. *Behold, I was shapen in iniquity; and in sin did my mother conceive me.* Psalm 51:5

Childish desires are selfish ones, so parents must channel these energies into acceptable outlets. Without proper adult intervention, children would grow up to be evil, using whatever means they could to satisfy their own desires. This belief in original sin is the closest perspective to the Christian view-point.

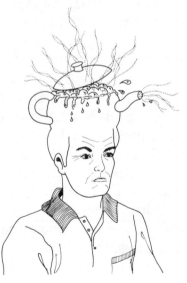

Some people are like over-heated kettles, boiling over with earthy desires and aggressive instincts. Parents need to keep children away from their evil impulses and direct them to behave appropriately.

We live in a violent world. Each and every day people everywhere bubble over with violent tendencies. Because violence has inflicted itself on our society, many experts want to know what exactly is aggression, and how do we learn it? Is the tendency to be violent part of human nature, or is it something we learn?

What Is Aggression?

If a small child is being picked on by a bully and the smaller child fights back, some people might consider both children to be out of line. Others might feel that only the bully is the aggressor, and the small child is acting in self-defense.

Is the tendency to be violent something that we are born with, a basic part of human nature? Some experts believe that people have aggressive energy. When levels of aggressive energy become critical, persons then act violently to release the aggression. If being hostile is instinctual, then we are violent because we are born with the tendency to be violent and destructive. This energy could be released appropriately through working hard or playing. When energy doesn't find an acceptable outlet, people vent their hostility through insulting others, fighting, or destroying things that belong to other people. Persons who turn their aggressive urges inward become those who punish or mutilate themselves and sometimes commit suicide.

The Cat Takes the Rat?

A remarkable experiment conducted in 1930 by Kuo, proved that cats may not be instinctive killers of rodents. Most of the literature available suggests that cats kill rats. Kuo raised kittens either by themselves, with rat-killing mothers, or with rats as companions. Eighty-five percent of the kittens raised with rat-killing mothers became rat killers. But only 45 percent of kittens raised alone became rat killers. Of the cats who were raised with rats, 175 of those became rat killers. The results of the kitten and rat experiment suggest that social learning can change or even *eliminate* behaviors that are often dismissed as instinctive.

Hostility—What's In It For Me?

Once a child behaves aggressively why does he continue to do so? For many adults and children aggression is a means of achieving an end. For example, a toddler may learn that snatching a toy away from someone is a quicker and more effective means of getting the toy than waiting for a turn. It's also quicker than negotiating to get the toy. Aggression is also rewarded in our society in several contexts. Those in military service, football players, and policemen all can win medals, trophies, or commendations for performing aggressively. Do such rewards reinforce aggression? Some believe "Yes," others say "No."

Violent tendencies are also maintained if they are a means of self-protection. Children who are street-smart know that fighting back is one of the best ways to keep from being attacked. Children who withdraw or cry when they are attacked are more likely to be attacked again.

If they are the quickest means to an end, if they are acceptable in certain social contexts, or if the behavior is used for self-protection, violent behaviors will continue in our society.

Age and Aggression

Are 3 year-olds are more aggressive than 8 year-olds? The nature of their aggression greatly changes with age. Florence Goodenough conducted one of the best studies on how aggression changes between ages 2 and 5. Some of her test results include the following discoveries:

- the number of temper tantrums tapered off between 2 and 5 years and were uncommon after age 4.

- younger children did not sulk or whimper as much as the older children following aggressive behaviors.
- children over 3 years would fight back more when attacked or frustrated.
- the 2 and 3 year-olds were most aggressive after being frustrated by their parents or an authority; older children fought more with friends or siblings.
- younger children stamp and hit more when they are frustrated, while older children used more verbal aggression, such as name calling.

Younger children fight over toys or other material things. Older nursery school children fight over objects too, but they use more personally directed violence than younger children. In other words, the kind of aggression seen in smaller children is instrumental—aggression as means to getting a toy or other desired object. Older children don't fight over toys as much as small children; however, the kind of aggression older ones are more likely to use is hostile—aggression with the intent to harm another; the major motivation is hurting someone else, not merely as a means to get an object away from them. For example, if girl smacks her little brother to get a lollipop from him, the aggression is *instrumental*. If that same girl smacks her little brother and then calls him a cry baby (with no intent to take the lollipop), her aggression is *hostile*.

Younger children are not good at knowing when *hostility* is deliberate or accidental. They will respond in the same way to an aggressive act regardless of intent. If a child is accidentally tripped by another child, he thinks the tripping was deliberate. Older children are better at recognizing *intent* in an aggressive act. They will not automatically go kick someone who kicked them by accident.

Once Aggressive, Always Aggressive?

Some children have more scrappy personalities than other children. If a child is full of fight as a preschooler, will the child be very aggressive throughout his school years and into adulthood?

The kinds of aggression seen in children and adults are different, so we are really comparing the persistence of aggression, whatever the form. Common forms in children include hitting and fighting, threats, teasing, and competitiveness. Common adult forms include the tendency to lose one's temper when frustrated and competitiveness.

Aggression levels are quite stable from preschool age through preadolescence for both boys and girls. Though it takes on different forms, an aggressive 5 year-old girl is likely to be an aggressive 10 year-old. It is common for aggressive levels to drop off for girls in adolescence, while remaining stable for boys. The reason for this decrease aggression for adolescent girls might be that rough-and-tumble, tomboyish behavior is allowed for girls while in grade school, but society expects more genteel behaviors from young ladies. Boys continue to be rewarded for their aggression well into their teen years.

Guns and Soldiers versus Dolls and Dishes

Boys are likely to remain more aggressive than girls because they are more aggressive in the first place. The kinds of aggression observed in boys and girls varies as well. Girls are more likely to use verbal aggression, while boys use more physical aggression.

One reason girls are less aggressive is that they are not targets for aggression as often as boys. The simplest explanation for this is that, in our society, boys are taught from little on up not to hit girls. Traditionally, boys receive more encouragement for being aggressive. For instance, parents purchase guns, soldiers, and other weapons for boys, while many parents give girls dolls, dishes, and things of that sort. Boys are also encouraged more than girls to fight back, because our society still considers fighting to be a masculine behavior.

What Are We?

Boy or girl, young or old, what lessons we learn as we grow up will best determine what kind of person we are—violent or warm and cooperative. Some important factors that determine what we become include culture, social class, our upbringing, and exposure to violent media. The United States is the most violent, stable democracy in the world. The percent of violent crimes (rape, robbery, murder, and assault) is very high. Maybe it is not a coincidence that the United States also boasts the most violent TV programming of any Western nation. The culture that one lives in effects overall levels of aggression.

In the United States, social class influences levels of aggression in children. Children from lower social classes

are more likely to be aggressive than children from the middle or upper classes. Mothers from different social classes rely on different kinds of punishment. Middle-class mothers use more psychological punishment, and lower class mothers resort to more physical punishment. This may help to explain why lower class children are more aggressive. When children are physically punished for being aggressive parents provide exactly the kind of role model that encourages more aggression in the future. For instance, if a child is smacked for doing something that his parents don't like, that child is more likely to smack a friend or sibling who does something that he doesn't like.

Warm or Cold?

Do the studies support that children are less aggressive when raised in a warm, loving atmosphere or a cold, rejecting atmosphere? Parents who tend to be cold and stand-offish with children will produce more hostile offspring than warmer parents. For one reason, cold parents are less likely to support a child's dreams and goals. That can be very frustrating to children, who may respond with hostility because their needs are not being met. Secondly, colder parents don't encourage their children to develop loving responses that might control a hostile outburst. Surprisingly, children also are more willing to learn ways of controlling their aggression from warm parents than from cold ones. Parents who express concern for their children consistently and warmly tend to raise children who are outgoing, friendly and less aggressive.

Blame It On The TV

Since children learn aggressive behaviors through observing them, does aggression on TV or in movies serve to increase their aggressive levels? Children in many Western nations can simply turn on the television anytime during the day and see violence. Such a question is well-worth considering.

3
The Role Of The Media

Some forms of forceful physical energy are not considered violence: an all-out tennis match, men laying railroad track, racing horses . . . But change the circumstances somewhat: a hockey game in which a difference of opinion is debated by fists and hockey sticks; bandits shooting at the railroad men; one jockey trying to force another off the track . . . These are violent.[1]

What Is Violence?

"The overt expression of physical force against others or self, or the compelling of action against one's will on pain of being hurt or killed. The expression of injurious or lethal force has to be credible and real in the symbolic terms of the drama. Humorous or even farcical violence [The Three Stooges] can be credible and real, even if it has a presumable comic effect. But idle threats, verbal abuse, or comic gestures with no real consequences were not to be considered violent,"[2] explains George Gerbner, Dean of the Annenberg School of Communications at the University of Pennsylvania.

In a 1981 newspaper interview when asked about increased violence on TV, ABC Television's president James Duffy said, "I see more action. Some people might call it violence—it's a matter of definition. But you can't have a screen full of people standing still."[3]

27

A brief examination of these two definitions of violence—specifically pertaining to the media will show you why this has become such a controversial issue. These authors agree with Gerbner's definition, simplified to state that **an act is violent that deliberately intends injury or death to another person.**

Violence All Around Us

Our national history is full of wars, rebellion, and crime. America has seen its share of civil turbulence, racial hostility, class conflicts, and terrorism. Our cities have steadily climbing crime rates, and even small towns cringe under the shroud of violence that possesses our society. Our youth are growing up in troubled times. No matter how hard we try, we cannot escape violence . . .

Consider for a moment how many violent acts the average child might be exposed to on a daily basis. Let's assume that the child is 10 years old with a morning paper route. As he folds the newspapers to be delivered, he scans a few headlines: THREE HOSTAGES KILLED IN TERRORIST HIJACKING; LOCAL MAN ARRESTED FOR GIRL-FRIEND'S MURDER; CLERK WOUNDED IN MINI-MARKET HOLDUP. Perhaps the child watches a couple cartoons before going to school, and sees Wile E. Coyote try to blow up the Roadrunner just after an anvil has fallen on the coyote's head. Then the child watches Popeye swing Brutus around by his hair before Brutus goes flying into the air and lands on his head. At school, a couple of kids take a few swings at each other during recess, and one

28

ends up with a black eye. As he's boarding the school bus, a child behind our paper boy is tripped by some older kids. The teacher on bus duty grabs the mischievious kids by the scruffs of their necks and hauls them back

into school. While the child waits for dinner to be ready, he watches a *Batman* rerun. Batman and Robin battle the villain and his henchmen. POW! ZOOF! BAM! flash on the screen as the punches fly. After dinner, he sits with his parents and watches the evening news—more fighting, killing and rioting around the world, before settling in with with this week's episode of *Miami Vice:* Crockett is gunned down. The dying Crockett has violence flashbacks while his friends desperately try to shoot his attacker. The paper boy goes to bed knowing that tomorrow will be almost the same as today—violence and more violence!

Kinds of Violence

Violent crime and prime-time violence are not Americans' only exposure to violence. Police use violence, often to deter violence. Armies and soldiers use violence. Violence has many labels. Sometimes it is called "force" when used by those on the right side of the law. It can be called retaliatory action, or self-defense—any number of things.

One reason that violence is on the increase might be the accessibility of guns in this country, including handguns and mail order weapons. In England where gun laws are much stricter, the murder rate in its largest city is 1 in 65,000. In Detroit, the murder rate is 1 in 2,500.

All kinds of violence are readily seen on TV and in movies, where the different kinds of violence come into and out of fashion. Before the Vietnam War, war pictures and programs were more popular. Today the police/detective crime drama is most fashionable, however, interest in war pictures is on the rise. Almost all children have been exposed to TV violence. Why do some children react in certain ways to their exposure and others do not?

How children are affected by screen violence depends on several factors that come into play simultaneously. These factors include age of the child, his patterns of viewing, peer pressure, quality of family life, his socioeconomic status, his parents' involvement in his viewing and his own personlity, in fact, even his self esteem.[4]

Self-Esteem and Screen Violence

How screen violence affects children depends in part on their self-esteem. A child's self-esteem is the result of many variables, and in turn will affect many aspects of his life. *Studies consistently show that adolescents with low self-esteem tend to feel more anxiety than others. A child may have low self-esteem because he was severely punished, dominated or rejected by parents or others important to him.*

Low self-esteem can damage a child's ability to interact with others. He suffers more self doubt, anxiety and inferiority. Someone of low self-esteem is less capable of rejecting pressures to conform and more susceptible to outside influences. *People with high self-esteem can better resist pressure to conform because they believe in their own perceptions, express their views and interact better with others.* Any outside influence, such as TV and film, are more likely to affect the child of low self-esteem.

Studies have shown that low esteem children are more susceptible to TV in particular because they watch more TV. **Studies on family relationships have shown that high esteem children get along better with their parents than low esteem children. As a result, they spend more time doing things with their parents. High esteem children spend more time on hobbies and with friends.** Their varied interests keep them occupied. They don't need TV as something to do the way that low esteem children do.

Education and intelligence seem to play a part in self-esteem. High esteem subjects tend to be better thinkers and are more articulate. High esteem children can better discuss screen content that disturbs them, which helps reduce their level of disturbance. Low esteem subjects are less likely to find a way to reduce the disturbance they feel caused by screen violence.

Because they lack meaningful involvement with family and friends, low esteem children not only watch more TV, they also prefer the TV shows and movies that are not close in content to their real life experience. It may be that they are not very happy in their real lives, therefore they like programs that are as far removed from that as possible. High esteem viewers are more interested, in contrast, with more realistic programs and are not as affected by things that don't relate to their own experience.

High esteem children can better make the distinction between fantasy and reality. If they see something on the screen that disturbs them, they have more ability to put that program into context with their other life experiences. Low esteem subjects will be more upset by a television program because they confuse fantasy with reality and they have fewer chances to test and construct "reality through interaction with others."

Age and Screen Violence

A child's age is an important factor in whether he will be strongly affected by screen violence. Younger children watch TV more than older children. The U.S. National Commission on Causes and Prevention of Violence issued a statement in 1969 that concluded, "A constant diet of violent behavior on TV has an adverse effect on human character and attitudes."[5] **One reason that small children have trouble digesting all the violence in TV and movies is that they are often too young to understand the context in which it is used. They simply do not have the thinking skills to evaluate violence within a framework. Unlike adults, young children cannot analyze plot, the nature of the conflict, and characterization to determine how the violence points up these contextual elements.** Violence is in the eye of the beholder. The young child will not understand why the violence is happening and may see violence for violence's sake only.

Violence on TV is not going to go away. Ratings show that it attracts viewers. Parents would do best to ensure their children, especially small children, are not watching TV in a vacuum. Parents should not only help guide children in their viewing choices, they should also take time to explain things on the screen that a child cannot understand. Parents can help children express their feelings about something they have seen on TV, particularly if it has disturbed the child.

It is necessary to explain why some outlaws on TV are treated as heroes because they commit crimes. Otherwise a child might be left to conclude that if they steal from the rich and give to the poor, they will be a hero, just like Robin Hood.

Children are also more vulnerable to the cinematic techniques the movie makers use to simulate violence. Close-ups, camera angles and sophisticated film editing make filmed violence more graphic and larger than life. A child can become terrified if he is able to sympathize with the victim. When the victim is another small child, as in *Jaws*, the experience can be most horrifying. Recent research on the effects of TV viewing in America showed that constant repetition of violent acts in crime series has created such an empathy with TV victims, that people have more fear and mistrust of other people than ever before. That fear is amplified in small children.

Children are capable of being influenced to behave aggressively by authority figures, such as parents, teachers, powerful friends, even screen personalities that they admire. Some researchers believe there is more danger in a child watching his favorite TV star commit casual violence on every episode than in exposing the child to gory, violent horror movies. If the child identifies with a good guy (policeman, cowboy, detective) who is always using casual violence, the child is more likely to imitate this TV idol than some giant green half-man half-monster. Also, how can children understand that we can't solve our problems with violence, when they see daily examples of it on TV? It is important for parents to take an active part in helping a child sort out what he sees on TV with what is expected of him in life. In life you cannot turn the corner and shoot someone just because you are basically a good person with good intentions and the other person is bad, deserving of pain.

Screen Violence and How Children Learn

Children learn through observation and imitation. It is a simple and natural way for them to learn. If you put your hands in front of your eyes, a small child will put his hands over his eyes. If you take your hands away to say, "Peek-a-boo," so will the child.

Observing behavior is the first step in learning a new behavior. Then the child tries to imitate what he sees. If his attempt is reinforced by a parent or teacher, the behavior is learned. Children can learn to imitate from watching many sources, they learn from real-life models (parents), from symbolic models (teachers, coaches) and from representational models (people on TV and in movies). Most of the social and antisocial behavior that children display is learned from imitating models. In the cases of antisocial or deviant behavior, often the model is acting in a way the child has never seen. If the child is emotionally aroused, the likelihood of his imitating that behavior increases. Children can be aroused through stressful situations and, of course, through drug use. For example, assume that a child sees another child on TV (a representational model) slap his mother. If the child has never been told not to slap his mother, next time he is fighting with his mother, he may in imitation of the model slap her. More than likely the child has been told, "You don't slap your mother," at some point in his young life. If he sees the model slap his mother, that action weakens his inhibiting response and can result in a slap later. This can release other aggressive behaviors previously stored by the child.

Since 98 percent of all households have at least one TV turned on an average of 6 hours a day, it is not unlikely that a lot of children are getting their socialization from the tube and not from their parents.

Whether or not researchers agree on the dangers of watching TV violence and its direct effect on viewers, TV, itself, is not harmless. Some TV programs present the kinds of activities through which children learn best how to be valuable members of society. **When the TV is on, that means the family is not talking, playing games, engaging in festivities or having discussions.** A child needs all of those activities. That is how his learning takes place and how his personality and character are formed. Turning on the TV can turn off the process that transforms children into people.

4

The Hunter, The Hunted, & The Spectator

Not all of the violent entertainment that we watch will damage our minds and and turn us into strong-armed barbarians. *Hamlet* and *Macbeth* are, after all, quite violent, yet these are not banned. Reading historic accounts of the violent acts committed by the English kings, Roman emperors, and the Christian crusaders is not thought to influence us adversely. And, who would dare say that "Jack and the Beanstalk" should not be

read to children? Some people would, however, namely because Jack was a rather nasty boy who trespassed on the giant's property, and robbed him of the hen that laid golden eggs, a talking harp, and bags of diamonds. Then, Jack killed the giant when he tried to reclaim his property.

Others believe that rather than harm us, the fictional violence of literature and the real violence of history is meant to entertain and teach us. One reason that we are not substantially affected by these stories is that we are far removed from them.

"After reading *Macbeth*," writes author Patricia Marks Greenfield, "my daughter, Lauren, went to see Roman Polanski's film of the play. Although she had read about Macbeth's severed head at the end of the play, it was a shock to see it in the film. She commented that she had not realized there was so much violence in the play. Her response is probably similar to those of children studied in England twenty-five years ago: more than twice as many said they had been frightened by things they had seen on television or film than in reading or radio."[1]

The visual media is a powerful force. When we read descriptive passages in a book, we are limited by our own imagination as to the extent of the pictured violence. Consider for a moment the word "hit." You have now seen it in print—What visual images immediately pop into your mind? Perhaps a flat-handed slap? Now think of the various horrible possibilities of the word. Form the hand into a fist and the violence becomes more extreme, add a body part receiving the action (the head) and visual images become clearer. However, it still takes much more imagination on the part of the reader to interpret words into dreadful pictures. The video media removes this restraint, and in a 30 second shot we are confronted with images more extreme than we ever could have dreamed. The "hit" now becomes a bloody scene of personal injury. We are forced to view the jarring impact, the rushing blood, the yielding of teeth, and finally the loss of consciousness. "Doesn't sound so bad," you say? That is a second problem with media violence. We see it so often and with gradually more severe consequences that it doesn't bother us any more. The things that we see all of the time on TV, in effect, cause us to become "used to" violence. Our comment may be "That really looked fake," or "That was a good stunt." We don't think of the pain that would be caused by a violent action in real life.

Apathetic Viewers

Drabman and Thomas (1974) tested children's response to a situation in which two younger children behaved aggressively toward one another. Twenty-two male and twenty-two female third and fourth graders viewed either an aggressive cowboy film or no film, then were left in charge to watch over two younger children whom they could see via a TV monitor. The prepared video tape showed the children playing quietly then becoming progressively aggressive toward one another and destructive to property. Researchers measured how long it took the subject to seek adult help after the aggressive behavior began, and whether the subject intervened before the youngsters abused each other physically. Drabman and Thomas found that relative to the no film group, the boys and girls who saw the aggressive cowboy film took longer to seek adult help and were much more likely to tolerate all but the more violent physical aggression and destruction before seeking help. 58 percent of the no-film group went for help, and only 17 percent of the children in the film group responded at the same low level of aggression. These findings supported the claim that TV violence makes young viewers apathetic to real-life violence.[2]

Children Believe What They See

Adults know that they are watching actors and that after the scene, the actors get up and go about their business. Children don't have that same privilege. They view what is on television or a movie as being real. And, the closer the setting is to real life—the more convinced they are. Children and a large number of adults believe that what they see on film is a reflection of what is happening in society. It is with this fact in mind that we take a good look at what television and other media are teaching about violence.

Violence Is Popular

"TV violence teaches children to be aggressive, to solve interpersonal problems through physical violence," says Dr. Leonard Eron, professor of psychology at the University of Illinois at Chicago. "They see that law enforcement officials, good guys, bad guys—everybody uses violence. It becomes an accepted way of behaving."[3]

An evaluation of fifteen hundred boys aged thirteen through sixteen showed that those who had watched a lot of television were nearly 50 percent more likely to commit serious violent acts than boys who didn't spend much time in front of the TV. Certain programs were more likely to lead to serious violent behavior than others; among the worst offenders were those which featured physical or verbal abuse in close personal relationships, programs with gratuitous violence not arising out of the plot, realistic fictional violence, violence done by "good guys" and violent Westerns.[4]

I'm Not To Blame

Any producers of children's entertainment would piously swear that nothing could be farther from their intention than to instill in young people a scorn of law and order. Yet, in the guise of drama, boys and girls are taught that the end justifies the means and that justice is what they say it is. Among the number of films and TV programs designed for adult viewing that were popular with children are the James Bond series and *Mission Impossible.* Bond, armed with a collection of deadly, incredible weapons, goes forth to battle evil. Because he is on "our side" and supported with unlimited wealth by a governmental department, his unawareness of civil rights of those who stand in his way and his heartlessness are depicted as part of his dedication to the cause. *Mission Impossible* uses extralegal means (wiretapping, kidnapping, drugging) to combat evil and achieve worthy ends. These are both spy adventures which go about breaking the law for a higher goal. If we want our children to respect the rights assured to us by the Constitution, these stories don't seem to be the most effective way of doing it. Even Herbie, the "lovable Volkswagen" careens into unoffensive citizens, demolishes property, and teaches our children to ignore rules, traffic lights, signs, and other evidences of restraint. Children identify with the James Bonds, the *Mission Impossible* crew, Herbie, and the multitudes who are indifferent to society's codes.

Good Guys' Violence

Televised violence teaches that violence is an acceptable and normal method of solving problems. In fact, the message is that shooting, stabbing, and slugging are far more efficient and work better than more time-consuming techniques such as reasoning, logic, or understanding. This is contrary to what Jesus was teaching when He said, *Blessed are they which do hunger and thirst after righteousness: for they shall be filled. Blessed are the merciful: for they shall obtain mercy . . . Blessed are the peacemakers: for they shall be called the children of God.* Matt. 5:6-9

In almost all television programs with a violent content, particularly police or detective stories, peaceful options

41

such as patience, understanding, compassion, or due process of law are not important, so long as the right side wins. When good guys use the same kinds of violence as the bad guys, the approval that their actions teach is a powerful anti-Christian lesson.

The Untouchables

One of the earliest of this type of television shows was *The Untouchables* which depicted struggles against gangsters. In a unique study of the effects of televised violence, a group of children was shown this program. Liebert and Baron offered the 5 thru 9 year-olds the opportunity to either help or hurt another child by pushing a button that made a handle the child was required to turn either easier to turn (a "Help" button) or that made the handle grow hot (a "Hurt" button). The children who viewed a violent excerpt from *The Untouchables* were more willing to hurt than were children who saw an exciting but nonviolent sports sequence. The results of this experiment and other similar experiments showed that television influences behavior in many ways other than imitation.[5]

The A-Team

In a more recent example, the message of *The A-Team* is that crime could be crushed if only the authorities would get out of the way of lean-and-mean specialists. The four superheroes are established as Vietnam veterans unjustly convicted of a crime they did not commit, who now live in hiding. Weekly, they emerge to defend weakling victims of gross injustice against their tormentors. This defense is accomplished through disguise, deceit, every type of action imaginable and violence of previously unknown varieties.

Wiseguy

Wiseguy was a new entry in 1987. Vinnie is a government operative being used to infiltrate and destroy organized crime. This, of course, he does with violence in excess of 45 acts per hour.

Commando and Invasion USA

Commando and *Invasion USA* are two movies that depict cases of heroes taking the law into their own hands. In the movie, *Code of Silence*, Chuck Norris uses a remote control tank and grenade launchers in his job as a Chicago policeman out to clean up the mob with 96 acts of violence per hour.[6]

Military Violence

NCTV reports that entertainment violence has been shifting toward a heavier emphasis on war brutality. A series of movies since 1984 dealing with military violence and revenge are guilty of glorifying violence and increasing the likelihood that viewers will turn to violence more readily in their own lives as well as support and demand military action in situations where such action may be undesirable. They also affect the viewer's attitude toward international events. *Uncommon Valor* in which a band of American veterans invades Vietnam to rescue secretly held prisoners of war started the trend of this type of movie. In *Missing In Action*, Chuck Norris rescues MIAs in Vietnam at the cost of 134 killings or attempted killings. *Rambo* set box office records around the world as Sylvester Stallone averaged 161 acts of violence per hour with Rambo killing Vietnamese and Russians in 58 separate attempts.

Rambo

Rambo III includes approximately 125 deaths and twice the violence of the previous movies in this series that glorifies war and hatred. "Rambo doesn't have a heart. He's a fighting machine and that's all," says one movie critic. "After all, a real man needs to go massacre hundreds of people every so often."[7]

While the *Bible* teaches that we must love our enemies and resist evil with good, hatred of the enemy is a clear teaching of *Rambo*. He hates the Vietnamese and Russians and says so. While Jesus Christ taught that it is even wrong to call another person "fool," Rambo uses the names "bastard" and "scum." While Jesus taught *he who lives by the sword will die by the sword*, Rambo is held up as a great American hero. No effort is shown in the film to even attempt to resolve problems in a non-violent manner.

Iron Eagle

Iron Eagle portrays a group of teenagers who arrange to "borrow" a couple of US military high-tech fighter planes and invade an Arab country in an effort to rescue the military pilot father of one of them. In the climactic scene, the young American fights the Arab leader in an action-filled dog fight and kills him. His punishment for his illegal actions—admission to the Air Force Academy, the answer to his dream.

Delta Force

In *Delta Force*, military violence is again distorted and glamorized as a highly successful and patriotic way of resolving international conflict. These movies mistakenly identify war violence with patriotism. They misunderstand that the purpose of our military is to keep us out of war, not to get us into war. They depict war incorrectly, as an exciting patriotic undertaking where Americans get a chance to prove that they are "real men" and kill enemy soldiers.

The glorious portrayal of a violent Chuck Norris as the perfect idol for hero worship is a disgrace to real American heroes like George Washington, Thomas Jefferson and Abraham Lincoln. Dwight D. Eisenhower said, "War is hell." These films contradict that leader's statement by showing war as exciting action where Americans need to fear little since they are almost impossible to hit, but the dirty enemy die left and right. These movies teach us to hate our enemy and crave revenge. They make it look exciting, easy and 'safe to use violence and murder as a way to deal with our frustrations.

The Vietnam War theme has frequently reappeared on television as well. Both Matt Houston and Thomas Magnum went back to Vietnam to "win one for America." **The moral being learned in America's living rooms is that good guys and bad guys both use violence, just make sure that yours is the more effective use.**

Due Process of Law

A study of 430 boys, aged nine to eleven years, revealed that the more television violence they witnessed, the more the child was willing to use force as a solution to conflict and to perceive it as effective. Social psychologist Fredric Werthan noted that children have absorbed from the mass media an idealization of violence: "Not the association of violence with hate and hostility, but the association of violence with the good and just—this is the most harmful ingredient."[8]

The Equalizer

Despite the American tradition of law and the Christian tradition declaring revenge to be misguided and wrong thinking, intense vigilante revenge violence dominates the media. *The Equalizer* has taken to the air waves to bring violent justice upon those who prey on the weak and

45

manage to elude the law enforcement officials or escape through a loop hole in America's judicial system. *Spenser for Hire* is another show where criminals and molesters are routinely killed, rather than trust their punishment to the system of law. *Lady Blue* depicted a violent female police officer who delighted in killing criminals even when she could arrest them nonviolently.

The message of prime-time American television is that taking the law into your own hands and settling problems with fists and guns is the best and only way to deal with conflict.

Death Wish, by Brian Garfield, is a book about an urban vigilante who goes about his rounds killing suspected muggers. The book and the subsequent movie version glorified the vigilante. The movie was seen by sell-out crowds which occasionally stood and applauded whenever Garfield's "hero" blasted away with his gun. *Death Wish* is classified as the first urban Western (certainly the first successful one) since the movie called *M*. CBS bought television rights and aired this film in '75-'76 season. Garfield offered to refuse $50,000 royalty payment if CBS would forgo showing the movie. He feared it would inspire imitation. CBS refused.

Cobra

Both *Cobra* with Sylvester Stallone and *Raw Deal* with Arnold Schwarzenegger feature heavy revenge themes in which the stars play murderous US police offiers who kill 37 and 42 opponents each. In 89 minutes Stallone kills five times as many people as the entire Miami police force did in all of 1985. *Cobra* repeatedly advocates the arbitrary police execution of offenders as the only way to solve society's crime problem.

Other recent revenge or vengence films are *To Live and Die in LA*, and *Death Wish 4*.

Violence for Violence's Sake

"This simple version of social responsibility ('crime does not pay') comes through the screen as a two-edged value. For one thing, crime on television is almost always exciting, intense, and even fun-filled. The bank robberies have a fascinating appeal, and to lead police in a high-speed automobile chase, particularly down slippery streets, always appears as nearly the ultimate in daredevil manliness."[9]

Media executives teach this perverted sense of socialization to our susceptible youth. **If crime does not pay, why does it appear that so many people on television and in the movies are having so much fun committing it?** Violence is also presented as a demonstration of power. It is the way one gets power and the way one keeps power. When viewers see a character that they enjoy watching use violence to solve a problem, they accept violence as the preferred method to solve problems that confront them.

Why do the makers of these films and the producers of the suspect television programs feel the need to include vividly violent scenes in their products? "To the studios, violence is an insurance policy of sorts. They feel that if you have violence two thirds of the way through, if a film seems to be lagging maybe you'll pick the audience up for the last third," states Peter Yates, director of *Bullitt, The Deep, Breaking Away,* and *Elenji.*[10]

What Mr. Yates is describing is simply inserting a little violence "for viewer interest." Using violence for violence's sake is the worst misuse of the media yet. Again, spy movies, crime, detective, and police shows are the biggest offenders. James Bond films are especially guilty. Here violence is portrayed as justified, necessary, very successful, and heavily rewarded. *The Living Daylights* is the most recent in this string of movies where James performs large amounts of violence with the air of supreme self-righteousness and omnipotence. It is interesting to note that whereas Bond movies are considered family entertainment in the US, they are restricted to adult viewers in England and banned entirely in Sweden.

NCTV cites the *Dirty Harry* movies as well as the more recent *Murphy's Law, The Sicilian,* and *Penitentiary III* as prime examples of violence simply for the sake of violence. In the early days of TV, the writers for the detective series *Man Against Crime* received instructions stating: ". . . other crimes may be introduced [but] somebody must be murdered, preferably early, with threat of more violence to come . . ."[11]

Mattel's new *Captain Power and the Soldiers of the Future* has been classified as a massive indoctrination in the philosophy of violence. Mattel's message is that our enemies are inhuman and hopelessly evil. They can only be dealt with through killing.

Other television fare that is excessively violent: *Houston Nights, Private Eye, Beauty and The Beast, Crime Story, Hunter,* and *Sledge Hammer!*

NCTV worst films of 1987 for senseless or excessive violence:

1. The Running Man
2. Masters of the Universe
3. Fatal Beauty
4. Death Wish 4
5. Robocop
6. The Sicilian
7. The Hidden
8. No Where to Hide
9. The Living Daylights
10. Extreme Prejudice [12]

Dr. Martin Luther King spoke out against violence in entertainment in 1963 saying, "By . . . our readiness to allow arms to be purchased at will and fired at whim; by allowing our movie and television screens to teach our children that the hero is the one who masters the art of shooting and the technique of killing . . . we have created an atmosphere in which violence and hatred have become popular pastimes."[13] This is still true today.

5

Hooked On Violence

Dad's been hard to live with lately. He refuses to help the children with their homework, slams the table with his fist when someone crosses him, and is just plain cranky. It could be the kind of TV programs he's been watching. For years, psychiatrists have suspected that adults are as susceptible as children to TV's up or down mood effects.

You Are What You "See"

People's homes, rather than a laboratory, were chosen as the sites of an experiment by Roderic Gorney, psychiatrist at UCLA. One group of volunteers was assigned a steady diet of TV violence. Another group Gorney ordered to stick to "helpful" programs like *Medical Center, Little House on the Prairie,* and *Lucas Tanner.* Group No. 3 watched light entertainment. Group No. 4 received a mix of helpful and violent programs, and Group No. 5 received complete freedom to choose what it wished.

The viewers recorded their feelings, and researchers independently interviewed each wife about her husband's behavior during the TV test period. The men who viewed helpful programs reported a noticeable drop in their aggressive feelings as the week progressed. The violence watchers reported no such relief. Most importantly, the wives declared that Group No. 1, the violence-viewing men, was the crankiest and most antagonistic. Of all five groups, the viewers of helpful programs turned out to be the easiest to live with.[1] (Further explanation on page 93.)

Television is a way to learn aggression, found John Langone, but it all depends on who is watching what and how often. Professional soldiers and policemen, for example, who are trained to act violently on occasion do not go about beating people up as a matter of course. Nor do average adults, who occasionally watch violence on TV, run out and murder or assault someone.

However, studies have proven that everyone—adults and children alike are affected to some extent by their choice of regular media diet.

Acting It Out!

Concern over whether children might copy what they saw on television sparked several studies which demonstrated that young children acquire novel aggressive behaviors from as few as a single viewing of a brief television or film portrayal. In one experiment, preschoolers saw a model perform a sequence of highly novel verbal and physical aggressive acts toward an inflated Bobo the Clown doll (a large light-weight plastic toy which has sand in the bottom so that it will bounce back when punched). The children were assigned randomly to groups which viewed the aggressive behavior performed by a live human model, a film of the live model, or a film of a costumed model that resembled a cartoon. There was a fourth, control,

group which saw nothing. After the viewing, the children were allowed to play in a room containing a Bobo doll, many of the same toys the model had used to attack the doll, and a variety of additional toys. Compared to the control group, all three groups displayed sharply higher levels of aggressive behavior. The children who saw the cartoon simulation showed slightly less aggression than those who had seen the live model or the film, but generally the differences among the three groups were negligible. Films of some of the children's post-viewing behavior reveal almost perfect imitations of the model's actions.

The results of this test showed quite a bit of spontaneous imitation for the children who had seen the model either rewarded or receive no consequences, but the children did not readily imitate the acts of the model whom they had seen punished. Also, boys displayed considerably more imitative aggression than girls.

In addition, there is clear evidence that although the child may fail to perform observed behaviors, he may nevertheless have learned them, and will use them later. Hicks found that when preschoolers were provided with a reward, they could recall and perform as much as 40 percent of the model's aggressive actions as long as eight months after viewing.[2]

Children Imitate Others

Over the past 20 years, researchers have focused on several processes to explain the learning of aggression. According to advocates of observational learning, children learn to behave aggressively by imitating violent actors on television just as they learn educational and social skills by imitating parents, teachers, peers, and others. Bandura's experiments pointed to the validity of this theory.

A number of researchers have attempted to determine the ages at which children are most susceptible to imitating observed behaviors. In two studies in 1973 and 1979, Collins and others consistently found that young children are unable to draw the relation between motives and aggression and therefore are more prone to imitate inappropriate aggressive behaviors. McCall, Park, and Kavanaugh reported that children as young as 2 years are quick to imitate televised behavior and some imitation is observed at even younger ages. Finally, a 1983 study by Eron, Huesmann, Fischer, and Mermelstein indicated that the period between 6 and 10 years is crucially sensitive for learning by observation. As for teenagers, Eron argues that once an individual reached adolescence, behavioral dispositions and inhibitory controls have become crystallized to the extent that the child's aggressive habits would be difficult to change with modeling.[3]

More simply stated, children can learn aggressive or violent behavior from any source at a very early age. These behaviors, once learned, are hard to eliminate, especially after the child reaches his teen years.

Reward or Not?

There are a number of factors that influence whether any source will be imitated. Again, a model who is rewarded is more readily copied, but a reward isn't always necessary.

The very fact that a violent act goes unpunished has the same effect. External characteristics are also a big influence on viewers. Obvious wealth, good looks, elegant dress and impressive titles lend the aggressive model great prestige and persuade the observer that the model is in full control of his environment and greatly encourages imitation. The observer assumes that he can use the same behavior to achieve similar effects. Natural resemblance between the observer and the model as to sex and age lead to imitation as does the belief by the viewer that the model is an expert in his field.

You can easily see why television and movies have such strong effects on viewers. Producers and directors deliberately create characters that encourage imitation.

Roots

The relàtion between television program material, viewer's attitudes, and viewer's later behaviors were demonstrated in Georgia by Rayback and Connel. The relative incidence of unruly behavior among white and black high school students was measured by the number of after-school detentions given to students in the time before, during, and after the broadcast of *Roots*. They indicated a significant increase for blacks during the weeks *Roots* was shown. Watching *Roots* apparently changed the black students' attitudes about obedience.[4]

Researchers have indicated that the more a program seems real, the more a viewer will believe its message and will want to imitate it. Newspapers frequently contain sad items about children who believe that the action-filled television life can be followed. The 14 year-old who hanged himself after watching rock star Alice Cooper on television, the nine-year-old who strangled himself on his cape while performing Batman leaps, the kindergartener who pushed his hand through a window, and the eight-year-old who lacerated his liver on his bicycle handlebars after imitating Evel Knievel, all have one thing in common: they followed through on their belief that what they saw on television was real.[5] Furthermore, they could do the same thing with little or no consideration of potential danger.

The Making of a Monster

Most research has associated childhood aggression with childhood exposure to violence. Does such bad childhood behavior predict adult criminal acts? The answer seems to be, "Yes." Boisterousness, hyperactivity, and even some "nastiness" may be related to violence viewing, but these are not the same as the antisocial aggressive behavior of youths and adults that concerns society. Evidence indicates that these childish types of aggressive behaviors are the predecessors of more serious antisocial behaviors of adults. A rapidly accumulating body of data suggests that aggression, as a characteristic way of solving social problems, usually emerges at a young age and remains relatively stable throughout a person's life.

Early Aggression Predicts Later Deliquency

870 children and their parents were interviewed in a 1960 study of aggression. In 1981 data was obtained on 542 of the original subjects which indicated that aggressive behavior is reasonably stable across time and situations. Also, children whose friends and classmates described as aggressive at age 8 exhibited serious antisocial behavior as an adult. The data suggests that aggressive habits are learned early in life and, once established, are resistant to change and predictive of serious adult antisocial behavior. If a child's observation of violence promotes the learning of aggressive habits, it can have harmful lifelong consequences.

It is such consequences that these authors are worried about. While media violence may influence only a small percentage of viewers, when the entire United States or the whole world is taken into consideration—that's a lot of violence! Could it be that those cute little children who used to run around imitating Batman's ZAPS and WHAPS are the ones who are now carrying submachine guns through the alleys of our major cities?

The Innocent Cartoons?
The most violent programming on TV is cartoons. Three times as many violent acts are committed in one 30 minute cartoon show as in the average prime-time hour-long dramatic program. Whether on cartoons or prime-time, the general lesson conveyed by television is that violence helps you achieve your goals (see chapter eleven).

TV is contributing to factors responsible for aggressiveness in our society through repeated messages that conflict is better solved through hostile behavior than by any other means. In short, the lesson that our children are taught is that violence is a way of solving problems.

In a study by Bandura, 88 percent of the children who saw an aggressive TV program displayed more violent behavior when allowed to play with toys after watching the program. They were free to play with non-aggressive toys such as crayons and farm animals, but chose to make weapons out of some toys.

Most children watch television an average of 26 to 33 hours per week. Anything or anyone that a child, or an adult for that matter, spends so much time with is bound to have a powerful influence over him. If he sees nothing but violence and abusive behavior or language, there is little hope that he won't be adversely affected. The message of television does NOT have to be one of violence. There is a wide range of programming available to us as parents. All that we have to do is choose for our children. Perhaps our choices will not be the same as his, but after all, we are the parents. It is our God-given duty to do what is best for our children. Let the magic screen's influence be one that you want for your daughter or son.

Make TV Work For You

Influences that teach children to be valuable contributors to society and to solve problems without aggression, must begin before children can read and write. We use the ability to read and write as an index of civilized behavior in our society. Consider that a child's basic social behavior (his civilization—learning to walk, talk, play, eat, interact with others, show appropriate manners and behaviors in different social situations) has already been accomplished by the time he learns to read. His behavior is well advanced by the time he is a skilled reader, so it is rare that what a child reads can have a major effect on his behavior. A child needs an early foundation of prosocial influences.

If more examples of prosocial behavior were shown on TV, more children might be inclined to exhibit this behavior. Consider the chart here. On the left, the type of prosocial behavior is listed. On the right are suggestions of activities showing that type of prosocial behavior in use:

Type of Behavior	Activity To Illustrate
Providing assistance	Someone giving a gift or a loan, giving instructions to another, offering physical assistance.
Controlling an aggressive behavior	Demonstrate an alternative to aggression in a frustrating situation. (talking a problem out, soothing someone's anger or hurt feelings)

Making up for bad behavior	Apologize or admit a mistake was made.
Sympathy	Verbalizing concern for others and their problems.
Explaining feelings of others	Teaching and explaining what other people think and feel.
Denying, resisting temptation	Resisting the opportunity to engage in a bad behavior that would be of some benefit to another.

These are all activities that could be shown in TV programs, but only a few programs opt for the prosocial message. Television is a powerful medium to children. If you don't curtail their viewing hours, use TV as a positive instrument for learning, rather than a means to teach aggressive behavior.

Why is Violence Popular?

Why does your child choose *He-Man* or *The Real Ghostbusters* over *Mr. Roger's Neighborhood?* Why does your 13 year-old return from the video store with a tape about Santa Claus slicing people up?

Aggression is a part of life. All babies are born with it but don't know what to do with it until they are taught. Children are fascinated with violence, counsels Dr. Anna Freud. She said that the young child must be taught to deal with his natural aggressiveness. "The urge to hurt and destroy must be suppressed and redirected . . . toward healthy competition and worthwhile accomplishments." While the child is learning to deal with his aggressive tendencies, it can be harmful for him to be exposed to violence and aggression in others.[6]

Recent television research indicates it is action rather than violence that attracts children to the screen. Therefore, programs can present many forms of action other than violent action without sacrificing popularity. Studies indicate that the same program presented in two versions, one violent, one non-violent were liked equally by the viewers. Therefore, excessive violence is unnecessary. Repeated opinion polls show that Americans want less, not more violence on television and in the movies, so why is violence prevalent?

Gerbner states, "A handful of production companies create the bulk of the programs and sell them to broadcasters, not to viewers."[7]

There is no inherent demand for violence in the art of writing entertainment shows for television. The demand is placed there by producers, who feel it is placed there by advertisers, who feel it is placed there by viewers. Often a writer will be asked to "put some action into the scene." He'll be told to add a little tension. Most writers go along with the menacing music and the broken glass—and ultimately the broken head—because that is the way the game is played. Mankiewicz and Swerdlow so describe the high-rolling game in which "the money from a successful series can create a pleasant life for creative people." So the cycle continues—the programs contain lots of violence and are viewed by lots of people. Advertisers pay lots of money for air time between the violent acts, and lots of money is made for salaries and profits. When complaints are made, network executives point to the cycle and claim that they are only "giving the public what it wants." The size of the audience seems to confirm that we like what we get.

Violence is Addictive

Violence is addictive. It can be entertainment of a high order and young people get hooked on it. When boys and girls are bombarded by the violence spewed from television and films, they can lose interest in dramatizations that pose problems resolved through thoughtful, sometimes laborious efforts of a peaceful nature. It is easier to identify with the action figure than the thinker. Violent action can be the result of thought insufficient to develop other solutions, and violence can be a glamorous form of escapism to children fenced in by regulations in every aspect of their lives. Children rejoice to see "fairness," good or right triumph over "unfairness," evil or wrong, but the depiction of violence can confuse them. It can persuade children that violence is the only appropriate or possible solution—whereas if a more critical analysis of the situation were made, any number of peaceful alternatives might be discovered. It confuses them by presenting the violent figures of the bad guys as more dashing, and more desirable to imitate.

We, as parents, exert one of the biggest influences on our child's choices of media entertainment. A teenager has to make judgements based on quality, but he cannot do that alone. To provide it parents must have good judgement themselves. If you watch trash, how are you going to develop your child's judgement?

6

The Frightened Viewer

Did you know that the average American child has watched the violent destruction of more than 50,000 persons on television by the time he's eighteen? It is no wonder that Dr. Milton Eisenhower's National Commission on the Causes and Prevention of Violence found that most children and adults who are heavy viewers of television express a greater sense of insecurity and apprehension about their world than do light viewers. It is what he calls the "mean world" syndrome.

"What is the difference between a violent television program and a traditional fairy tale filled with gory incidents and terrifying villains?" you may ask. The answer is that a fairy tale is generally read to a child while he or she

is sitting in the parent's lap. This closeness gives the child a feeling of security. The reading of even the most frightening incidents is in the voice of one of the most important and trusted persons in the child's life. That familiarity adds distance to the incident. Also, the child's questions can be answered, and mysteries can be solved as they occur. The parent can soothe any fears that may arise. On the other hand, most children view television when they are alone, frequently in a darkened room. Parents are often in another part of the home while murderers, monsters, and mayhem parade in front of their vulnerable youngsters.

Children as old as third graders believe what they see on television to be real. Joan Anderson Wilkins in *Breaking The TV Habit* tells of a little boy who was watching a war movie that featured a chase scene with World War II airplanes. His mother, upon hearing a loud crash, ran into the room to find her dazed son standing next to a broken television screen. The boy explained that he had been trying to see where the airplane had gone. It is the fact that children believe the horror and violence they see on TV are real that causes many youngsters to have trouble going to sleep at night or that sleep to be filled with vivid nightmares. Joan Wilkins also relates the story of her son Luke's refusal to go to bed without lights in his bedroom, the hallway, and the bathroom. After six months of this behavior, Ms. Wilkins discovered that, without her permission, Luke had watched the made-for-television movie *Salem's Lot*. It was fear of Barlow, the vampire in the movie, that was interrupting his sleep. Parents don't seem to realize that what children see and hear before their bedtime stays in their subconscious and becomes part of the sleep experience. **After watching a made-for-TV movie about a baby alligator that grew to monstrous proportions in a city's water system, children were afraid to take baths or go to the bathroom in the middle of the night. "I was afraid . . . the alligator might be in my toilet," whispered**

one little girl. Just as there appears to be a link between viewing violence on television and violent behavior, so there appears to be a link between viewing scary programs and frightened children.[1]

"Between the ages of seven and eleven, children frequently mention that violent TV scenes frighten and upset them," says Dr. Glenn Sparks of Purdue University in a recent interview in *Woman's Day*. "Children this age realize these scenes could really happen—and happen to them. They're not ready to cope with this yet. The availability of scary scenes has risen dramatically with the proliferation of cable TV and VCR's." Dr. Sparks added, "Many children who saw *Friday The 13th* or *Halloween* are afraid robbers will come and chop them up."[2]

In 1977 Temple University reported that children between seven and eleven years old who were heavy television viewers were likely to be scared often. They were fearful of the world at large, frightened that someone bad would come into their house, and afraid that when they go outside someone will hurt them. The Annenberg School of Communications reports, "A Ten Year Study Of TV Violence," confirmed that school children who were steady television viewers had an exaggerated sense of danger and mistrust. The study also found that television viewers are more likely to believe that police frequently use force and will shoot fleeing suspects.[3]

It is from the Boob-Tube "babysitter" that such impressions emerge. The writers and producers of television fare set the mixed bag of opinions about policemen that appear in our living rooms. Ben Stein interviewed many members of this elite group of Americans for his book, *The View From Sunset Boulevard*. Some of their comments were supportive of this hard working element of our society, describing policemen as "dedicated, capable and efficient." However, the majority of reported interviews netted responses such as "police are a disaster," "a paranoid in-group," "ineffective." They view police as "hassling" young people, being "owned by the Mafia," selling drugs and treating people badly in general. With such a mixture of opinion being presented on prime-time television, it is no wonder that our children and teenagers don't know whether to turn to the police for help or run from them in fear.

Data concerning this subject collected from 587 adolescents revealed that heavy television viewers in every case were more likely than light viewers to believe that a greater number of people are regularly involved in violence. Heavy viewers were also more likely to overestimate the number of people who commit serious crimes. Heavy television viewers felt that it was dangerous to walk alone in a city at night, even in one's own neighborhood. Adolescent heavy viewers also tended to express mistrust in people as well as the belief that people are selfish. They were more likely to say that people "are mostly just looking out for themselves . . . and that one can't be too careful in dealing with people."[4]

Another way in which television violence exerts its influence on children is through molding of children's attitudes. The more television a child watches, the more accepting is his attitude toward aggressive behavior. The more a person watches television, the more suspicious he is, and greater is his expectancy of being involved in real violence. Attitudes are characteristic rules, and explanations learned from observations of behavior. If a child's or adult's major exposure to community living occurs through television, his concept of society would be based on this observation. Evidence suggests that television violence can alter one's attitudes toward aggression and these attitudes in turn influence one's behavior.

The Frightened Adolescent

Scary TV programs and films were popular with 80 percent of the students interviewed in a study done of

7th and 10th graders from a Wisconsin school. 26 percent reported experiencing enduring fright reactions in the preceding year, and 55 percent recalled experiencing such reactions at age 6 and under after watching scary movies.[5]

Television viewing also seems to contribute to the adolescent's assumptions about law enforcement procedures and activities. Among those surveyed, heavy television viewers believed that police often use force and violence at a scene of violence. They had misguided conceptions of how many times a day a policeman pulls out a gun, and heavy viewers believed that police who shoot at running persons actually hit them.

In one college, 90 students were randomly assigned to watch small amounts of TV of a non-violent nature or high amounts of violent TV shows. The results indicated that viewers of either type of shows were much more likely to think that they would become victims of violence. Students who were low in anxiety at the beginning of the study became more fearful for their safety no matter which group they were in. For students who were already highly anxious at the beginning of the study, only the group seeing injustice winnning out had major increases in anxiety.

The Frightened Adult

Most television shows are set in the present or in a time within the memory of the viewers. Therefore, the world seen on TV, having the close resemblance to that of the viewer, lures adults as well as children into envisioning prime-time television to be an alternate reality. This shaded reality is the product of the thinking of television producers and writers about life. Crime provides the single most recurrent theme on prime-time television; and when these crimes occur, they are generally violent. In life there is a lot of shoplifting, income tax evasion, embezzlement, and driving while intoxicated, but on TV it's kidnapping, armed robbery, rape and murder that predominate. Also presented is a distorted picture of the criminal.

As Ben Stein writes, "In real-life murders, rapes, and so forth both victims and perpetrators are usually poor, minority-group people, apparently acting on sudden impulses of rage and anger. Robberies and muggings also are usually perpetrated by young minority-group males . . . the victim is often another ghetto dweller." Television most often presents crimes being carefully planned involving one well-to-do white person killing another well-to-do white person. "On *Baretta* even the junkies wear fresh clothing and sport recent haircuts," says Stein. "In the thousands of hours I have spent watching adventure shows, I have never seen a major crime committed by a poor, teenage, black Mexican or Puerto Rican youth, even though they account for a high percentage of all violent crime [in reality]." David Begelman, ex-president of Columbia Pictures, states flatly that all criminals on television are white because of pressure from lobbyists from various ethnic minorities.[6]

It is no wonder that so many Americans, especially older-Americans, are afraid to walk the streets, even in their own home towns. They begin to believe that criminals are everwhere. Anyone in a 3-piece suit is suddenly suspect. Women in tennis dresses are believed to be homicidal maniacs. Frauds abound. Paranoia sets in.

If TV violence has a negative influence on the way people perceive reality, then those most heavily exposed to TV viewing will see more danger in their environment than those doing lesser amounts of television viewing. While most researchers have expressed fear that television stimulates viewers to violent or aggressive acts, George Gerbner contends that the consequences of TV's symbolic world of violence may be much more far-reaching. Gerbner and his research associates have found that people who watch a lot of television see the real world as more dangerous and frightening than those who view little TV. Heavy viewers trust their fellow citizens less and fear the real world more.

Gerbner conducted an extensive examination of the difference between television "reality" and the reality of life as found in public attitudes toward the possibility of becoming the victim of violent street crime. The results showed that heavy television viewers are much more likely to overestimate the true dimension and dangers of crime. For light viewers (watching two hours or less per day) other variables such as education or newspaper reading may intervene to neutralize the impact of television viewing. For heavy viewers, however, television overrides even the impact of a college education. And, viewers under the age of 30 showed a greater tendency to believe television no matter how few programs they watched. Thus, media violence trains victims as well as criminals. Violence on television leads viewers to perceive the real world as more dangerous than it really is, which must also influence the way they behave. One of the questions on Gerbner's survey was: "Can most people be trusted?" The heavy television viewer was 35 percent more likely to check "Can't be too careful." When he asked viewers to estimate their own chances of becoming involved in some type of violence during any given week, the respondents provided further evidence that television can induce fear. The heavy viewers were 33 percent more likely than the light viewers to choose such fearful estimates as 50-50 or 1 in 10, rather than a more plausible 1 in 100.

Gerbner concluded, "The exaggerated sense of risk and insecurity may lead to increasing demands for protection and to increased pressure for the use of force by established authority. Instead of threatening the social order, television may have become our chief instrument of social control."[7]

Among those television males with identifiable occupations, about 20 percent are engaged in police work. In reality, the proportion runs less than 1 percent. Heavy TV viewers were 18 percent more likely than light viewers to overestimate the number of males employed in law enforcement. A 1983 prime-time study by the Media Institute, a research group in Washington, found an average of 1.7 overwhelming violent crimes per show programmed on ABC, CBS, and NBC. *The researchers also found that murders were more than a hundred times as frequent on TV as in real life.* These statistics support the Annenberg School of Communications study of adults which found that persons whose viewing habits center on crime shows are more likely to buy a dog, or even a gun, for protection, install new locks on doors and windows, and avoid what they consider to be unsafe sections of towns. "Crime in the streets" is very real in the living rooms of peaceful small towns all over America, and if the bank is robbed or the rapist races down the street pursued by a policeman emptying his service revolver, or if screeching car chases endanger everyone on the road for three hours every night, seven nights a week, is it strange that on leaving the living room those images have created a permanent fear in the viewer, wherever he may live?

7

From Glimmer To Goliath

What do Phoenix, San Antonio, San Francisco, Memphis and San Diego have in common? They all have the same rate of crime per 100,000 persons as New York City. In any of these cities your chances are 1 in 14 that you will be a victim of violent crime.[1]

Violence is seen everywhere. For those who live in big cities, violence is a way of life. One need only look out the window, around the corner, or down the corridor to encounter theft, assault, robbery, rape and murder. If it is a slow week for savagery, city dwellers can do what the rest of America does to witness violence: they can turn on the TV set.

Television Violence Is Dangerous

From earliest times, myths, fairy tales, poetry, and some *Bible* stories have dealt in violence—murder, rape, robbery, guilt, greed, fear, separation. The Greek tragedies feature violence between husband and wife, parents and children, brothers and sisters. Shakespeare created 116 violent deaths. Traditional fairy tales outdo them all, particularly in violence done to children! Countless people who grew up on scary fairy tales, radio thrillers, and comic and film gore are nervous about the generation now growing up on television violence— rightly so.

We as authors believe that television violence is more dangerous. One reason for this is that TV is present in 98 percent of all American homes and children have

73

unregulated access to it. Not only does the combination of "sight and sound" have particularly potent influence, but TV doesn't have the built-in shield of books where children are protected by their lack of reading skill. The adult who is reading to him will exercise judgement in choosing the story, and the child will imagine the action and attach meaning to the words according to his maturity. Violence in the theater has a "box-office barrier" which serves a two-fold purpose. Here the child must be a certain age and must pay for a ticket before he has access to disturbing images. None of this is so with television. Even the preschool child can experience murder, muggings, rape, and robbery by turning on the TV set in the living room, something every two-year-old knows how to do.

Violence is a staple in the American television diet. We show more violent and fewer prosocial programs during prime-time than any other country in the world. In 1975, the Mexican government banned more than 30 TV programs because they felt that they were encouraging violent and criminal behavior. The majority of the programs had been imported from the United States.

The effects of TV violence vary according to the program. Factual, non-glorifying documentaries such as *Holocaust* have been found to increase rather than decrease sensitivity to violence. However, when the purpose of the violence is entertainment or if violence is shown as a successful way to resolve a conflict, the results have been quite harmful. Research shows that some common effects are: visible increases in anger and irritability, loss of temper, increased verbal aggression, increased fear and anxiety, and a desensitization toward violence. Decreases in sharing and cooperation, increases in fighting, distrust and dishonesty as well as in depression, willingness to rape, and actual criminal behavior have all been found repeatedly.

What Is Happening To Our Children?

Studies of violence have been made in the United States and abroad by pediatricians, psychologists, educators, governmental bureaus, journalists, and research arms of the film and television industries. The results are often contradictory. Among the non-industry connected specialists there is universal agreement that violence in their entertainment compounds the effects of other forms of violence, and is not good for young people. There is lack of agreement as to how much damage is being done to children, but only as to the degree. Disturbed sleep patterns, increased hostility, and fearful behavior are only some of the harmful effects that have been traced to entertainmment violence.

"If your eight-year-old watches a lot of TV violence, you can predict that you'll shape him into an aggressive child," writes Dr. Randall P. Harrison in a publication of the American Academy of Pediatrics.[2]

And while the federal government's 1982 update of the Surgeon General's report concluded that there was, indeed, evidence that "excessive" violence on TV leads directly to aggressive and violent behavior among children and teenagers, that behavior as seen in the research laboratory obviously does not involve rape or murder, but rather ordinary childish aggression—pushing, shoving, hitting, and so on.

Aggression is largely a learned behavior. "If you accept that argument, then it is hard to deny that television is a way to learn aggression," states John Langone. He goes on to say that it depends on who is watching what and how often, but it is fairly obvious that a young, impressionable child who views several hours of unsupervised television every day will probably be affected adversely, given the high frequency of violence in both cartoon and adult programs.[3]

Sociologist Dr. Clain T. Appell of Brooklyn College, reports that of families she has studied, **60 percent have changed their sleep pattern because of television, 55 percent have altered their eating schedules, and 78 percent have used television as an electronic babysitter.** By the time the average child in a television household graduates from high school, he has spent more than 15,000 hours watching television, nearly 4,000 hours more than in the classroom. The average American child spends more time watching television than he spends in any other waking activity, as much as one third of his day in passive comtemplation of the television screen.

TV's Humble Beginnings

In 1926, television was used as part of a vaudeville act. A picture was sent from one side of the stage to the other, amazing the audience. Unfortunately, the TV set was so heavy that it fell through the floor of the stage. The first home TV set, demonstrated in 1928 had a screen 3 inches by 4 inches.

"In the early days of television, the medium was a dessert, something families shared after dinner,

after daily chores, after talk time, and after homework," writes Joan Anderson Wilkins, "But what started out as dessert in the 1950's has now become the whole meal from soup to nuts." Television was different during its early years. First of all, it was "live." The programs aired blatant mistakes in front of real audiences. There was a stronger code of programming ethics. Black-and-white TV was less realistic and appealing than today's color sets. There were fewer programs and channels. As a result, viewers spent less time with television.[4]

TV violence first became popular in 1956 and 1957 with the arrival of the adult western. Previously, there had never been more than one crime program in the Nielsen top 20 in any year. Television programming at its start was relatively nonviolent. Between 1951 and 1953 there was a 15 percent increase in violent incidents on the television screen. Between 1954 and 1961 violence increased a further 17 percent, due to the popularity of prime-time action adventures, to about 60 percent of all programs. By 1964, according to the National Association for Better Radio and Television, almost 200 hours per week were devoted to crime scenes, with over 500 killings committed on the home screen—a 90 percent increase since 1952.[5]

NCTV reports that the stalking and brutal murder of women continues to be a favorite theme of TV's violent programming, and prime-time television still averages 10 acts of violence per hour with an attempted murder every 30 minutes. 40 percent of all prime-time TV hours are made up of programs high in violence.

The most popular violent show in the 1987 Fall season was *Tour of Duty* which contained 61 acts of violence per hour. This was followed by *Sledge Hammer!* with 58 violent acts per hour, *Wiseguy* with 45, *The Equalizer* 40, and *Houston Knights* 36. In one 1987 episode of *The*

Equalizer there were 81 acts of violence including 10 murders and 5 attempted murders. In almost all of the violent programs, good wins only through violence. While the typical television police officer kills one to four dozen people a year, real-life police officers in the United States fire their guns an average of once every 27 years. At current rates, the average American will view 45,000 murders or attempted murders on TV by the age of 21.[6]

People Want Violence

Why did television programming become the hotbed of violence and crime that it is now? It is simple: people want violence on television. The rating system that controls what appears on national television indicates that the public regularly chooses violent programs over peaceful alternatives. Advertisers protest that they would gladly give the public "Pollyanna" round the clock if that is what people would watch. The presence of large numbers of violent programs on TV is due in part to the desires of certain advertisers to attract audiences made up primarily of male viewers.

The main purpose of watching television is to relax and be soothed, so why do viewers not choose soothing, relaxing programming? Why do they opt for programs filled with the most violent activities imaginable—deaths, tortures, and car crashes, all to the accompaniment of frenzied music? It seems that by choosing the most active programs possible, viewers are able to approximate a feeling of activity, sensations of involvement—the simulation of activity in compensation for the passive, one-way experience of television viewing.

How TV Avoids Appearing Self-Serving

TV programmers often claim that they are only providing what the public wants to see. This is

debatable. Through ratings polls, America informs the networks who claim to do little more than follow the ratings polls, record the results, and provide the public with more fare that is likely to receive high ratings. In truth, the ratings system is not democratic. The audience is merely used to empower the networks to act on the audience's behalf. In point of fact, the people polled have no power in the decision making, no ability to organize an opposition the network's program, and only programs that have commercial sponsors can be polled.

Another popular maneuver of the networks is to hire professional consultants from academic circles to help authenticate programs. Hiring experts to help produce more historically accurate kids' shows or miniseries also portrays the network as interested in the public's educational well-being.

Off and on, there is Congressional interest in how much violence is shown on TV. When one of the networks was going to be reviewed for prime-time violence, it countered with a report on the number of prosocial messages in one of their programs. However, none of the networks has ever volunteered a study on the antisocial messages conveyed in their programming.

Television is one of the strongest social support systems in the country that reinforces antisocial messages, a changing definition of violence depending on the user, and antifamily lifestyles. Because so many of the programs employ the all too familiar and overworked storylines, violence and sex will continue to be inserted into programming to stimulate audience interest. Violence will continue to be condoned if the "good guy" or the powerful are using it against the "bad guy" or the powerless. Antifamily overtones will continue to erode established values. Consequently, another generation of children will grow up watching the creative exploits of others rather than using their own imagination and acquiring a sense of accomplishment, not through watching, but by doing.

The Goliath

In the early days of television, programs were imitations drawn from its immediate predecessor, radio. Many important people in the movie industry predicted TV would fail because its tiny, boxy black-and-white image could not compete with the enchantment of the big technicolor screen. Potential investors wondered why any American family would pay $350 for a TV when $35 would buy them a fine radio at a time when radio was in its heyday. Even fledgling TV production companies weren't sure whether sponsors would pay the costs necessary for sets, props, equipment, and actors who now had to memorize lines rather than read them from a script. Could anyone from the early days of TV have ever predicted the scope of TV programming today, the astronomical sums advertisers pay, and the power with which TV has changed our culture?

A whole generation of Americans witnessed TV's humble beginnings and its struggle to establish itself as a profitable medium. Perhaps the public's collective memory of TV as the scrappy new kid on the block inhibits its ability to see the powerful, self-serving monster that the television industry has become. Some people might consider that they have more  important things to do than be concerned with the actions of those who have access to TV. That a whole generation of Americans have been weaned on TV has been a most

80

profitable phenomenon for some. The popularity of trivia games attests to the number of people who have acquired vast amounts of knowledge about TV from sitting in front of it hour after hour. Toys modeled after TV characters and figures is a multi-million dollar industry. Author Phillips' book *Turmoil In The Toy Box* (published by Starburst Publishers) attests to that fact.

Phillips and Robie conclude, "If Americans aren't going to turn off the TV, if parents aren't going to curb their children's viewing hours, then some of the more profound effects of the daily TV diet should at least be considered."

8
Geared For Guerrilla Warfare

"Although television is not taken very seriously, it should be. Five hours a day (authors Phillips and Robie say 9.5 hours), sixty hours a week for millions, television is merging with the environment. After all, the average 16 year-old has clocked more hours with the tube than he has spent in school. The *TV Guide* outsells every other magazine in the nation. It would seem that television, which grew up to be what it is today by accident, without long-range planning, has done something in the process, also by accident, to the nation. **Just as our car culture, our restless motoring, required drive-in restaurants and**

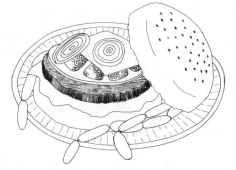

fast food franchises . . . filling stations of the stomach . . . so our developing TV culture requires fast food distraction, junk entertainment, psychic beef patties. The living room has been converted into a kind of car: the screen is its windshield; every home is mobile; everybody is in the driver's seat; and we are all seeing the same sights simultaneously," says former *New York Times* critic John Leonard.[1]

TV teens have a set of values dictated largely by Hollywood grownups. Certain values about families and children have been upheld in Western civilization for centuries. Traditionally, our society values raising children in a solid family unit. People who marry and stay married are recognized for their commitment. Our society expects people to care for their children. We have laws to protect children, and a legal system to prosecute fathers and mothers who abandon their families. The laws to protect marriage and family are enacted in a democratic society because they reflect the views of the mainstream. What could happen to these laws if the values change in that mainstream?

Soap Operas

Consider the values that are suggested to someone whose daily diet includes the soap operas. **Soap operas dispense with the value of real family commitment through the disposable marriage twist in many soap opera storylines.** Husbands, wives, lovers and children are here today and gone tomorrow. Soap opera characters are always falling into and out of love, divorcing, marrying or remarrying. As a result of the new wife, husband or lover, children are shuffled around, and often right out of the picture. A soap opera mother has a child one day, then somehow the child disappears. Children occasionally do become regularly featured characters, but it is more likely that they are rarely shown. The subtle message implied by not showing children on the soaps is that children are not important in family life today.

That children are rarely seen has in part to do with the fact that they are never brought into the world. On the soaps a disproportionate mount of babies are miscarried or stillborn. On that rare occasion that the baby does enter the world, it is usually in a highly dramatic fashion with the mother in a high risk situation. The best use of children in soap operas is to enhance the drama, to be both a danger and unfortunate prey in the parent's life.

Soap operas are also adept at using taboo subjects in storylines to excite and arouse viewers. Consider the incestuous overtones in some of the plots. A pair of lovers turns out to be half-brother and half-sister. An adolescent daughter falls in love with her father's best friend. Just when the story has its viewers most aroused, the screen flashes to a commercial about drain cleaner.

Clearly, the repetition with which tragedy strikes the soap opera characters results in desensitizing the viewer's empathy for human tragedy, rather than intensifying it. The most desperate circumstances are juxtaposed with dog food commercials and station identifications, so that any real involvement with the characters is stifled.

Though many soap operas now appear during prime-time, the prime-time shows are more renowned for chipping away at family values in other ways. One of the most popular illusions supported in prime-time is that men don't need women at their sides (or children for that matter). Many TV men get along fabulously in life without needing a woman or being needed by a woman. These men feel a long-term responsibility only to law and order, justice and their professions.

Some TV men live in a kind of emotional vacuum, while some shows picture men who develop a close family-type relationship with a co-worker or co-workers. As times change, TV features the independent woman whose own family is supplanted by a family of friends at work. If a TV show features a modern-day family living together and caring about each other, chances are it is a comedy.

Single Parent Homes

If the spouseless/childless lifestyle is a popular motif for adult shows, the parentless lifestyle is very popular in children's shows. The appealing message to kids is that having no parents means having no rules or boundaries and lots of freedom. The families that do appear in cartoons are either artifacts from a long time past *(The Flintstones)* or serve as a museum exhibit of the future *(The Jetsons)*.

Cartoons do not reinforce nurturing behaviors such as caring for sick children, feeding a baby, talking with a lonely or unhappy child—all of the typical behaviors for someone who takes care of children. Instead we are more likely to see kids playing or sleuthing around in gangs, unsupervised. The gang may be a bunch of teenage kids (Scoobydoo), animals, or superhumans. Regardless of the humanness of the gang, the young audience for these shows is asked to identify with kids who travel in bands unsupervised, or to view gang behavior as a desirable way of life.

The Power of the "Tube"

People in TV business know how to capitalize on the tube's ability to fashion our tastes for music, clothes and trends. A parent may think nothing of letting his child watch a mindless show that features child detectives who get into scrapes, but who also all play musical instruments and have a successful rock band. It is not common knowledge, but should be that all of the major networks have a vested interest in the kind of music that is played on TV. CBS, for example, has a musical instruments division that sells guitars and other items to kids who would like to start a rock group, imitating the rock groups on TV. The popular music that appears on kids' shows is there first and foremost to serve the self-interests of the networks who also control record companies and many recording labels and artists. By exposing kids to popular music through TV cartoons, the networks are whetting the musical appetites of many future record consumers.

TV As A Teacher

Television is a teacher, but do most of us realize exactly what it is teaching our children? Many families choose the location of their home based on the reputation of the school district. Parents want the best possible education for their children and constantly quiz friends and neighbors about teachers. Many handpick the best ones for their children each year. However, these same parents seem curiously unaware that when their children are not in school, many are learning a curriculum unfamiliar to the parents from a host of anonymous teachers on television. This curriculum covers every aspect of life, from the values children will follow to the jeans they will wear.

Television becomes a companion for many children today. Is the peer group that parents are choosing for their children one that they readily want emulated? Do we want our children copying the plastic lives of so many of the popular sit-coms that are on TV today? Are we being fair to our children by letting the television teach them that all of life's trials and tribulations can be solved within the one half hour time slot alotted such programs as *The Brady Bunch, Different Strokes, Silver Spoons, Who's The Boss?* and *Kate and Allie?* Do we want them to accept the single parent lifestyle as the prevailing norm due to the abundance of this type of programming?

What Is Real?

What effect does the constant intake of simulated reality have upon the viewer's perceptions of actual reality? Gross and Gerbner studied some of the effects of television "reality" upon people's ideas and beliefs pertaining to the real world. Their results suggest that the television experience significantly affects viewer's perceptions of reality. Heavy and light television viewers were asked mutiple choice questions about the real world. Accurate answers were offered with those that reflected a bias characteristic of the television world. The researchers discovered heavy television viewers chose the biased answers far more than the accurate answers, while light viewers were more likely to choose the correct answers.

For example, the subjects were asked to guess their own chances of encountering violence in any given week. The possible answers were 50-50, and 10-1, and 100-1. The statistical chances that the average person will encounter personal violence in the course of a week are about 100-1, but heavy viewers consistently chose 50-50 or 10-1 reflecting the "reality" of television where violence prevails. The violent television world distorts viewers perceptions of the real world and their expectations of violence in life reflect their exposure to violence on television.

Eyes That See Not

The heavy television viewers answered many other questions in a manner revealing that what they saw on television had altered their perceptions of the world and society. They overestimated the U. S. proportion of the world population and the percentages of persons employed as professionals, athletes, and entertainers just as television overemphasizes the importance of these groups. *Education of the viewer played no significant role in improving the distortions of reality produced by heavy TV watching.* College-educated subjects were just as likely to choose the biased answer as were those with only a grade school education.

It is necessary to note that the viewers' incorrect notions about the real world do not come from misleading newscasts or factual programs. They derive directly from repeated viewing of fictional programs performed in a realistic style within a realistic framework.

Is Prime-Time For Real?

Almost all real families with working parents depend on some form of child care and many families are struggling to make ends meet, particularly those headed by single women, reports The National Commission on Working Women which has published a study on fifteen situation comedies and eight dramas with children as characters. These were monitored for five weeks. Yet, **no single mothers on TV live in poverty or have economic problems. Additionally, no children lack essentials or extras. Serious race and sex discrimination don't exist. Bigotry is usually overcome by the end of the show, and young children are so self reliant that they don't need child care or the care is automatically provided by loving relatives or live-in help.**

TV also gives children an unreal perception of the world of material goods. Like the lesson of violence, the lifestyle of consumption isn't "taught" by television. It is simply picked up and absorbed by the viewer. Both the programs and commercials present an unrealistic view of the material world, one that represents a standard of living that most Americans will never attain. Television families confront unbelievable problems, but their material surroundings can be just as fantastic. Most homes on soap operas have felt the decorator's touch. One series of automobile ads featured people giving new cars to family members as gifts for such special occasions as an anniversary, a graduation, and a sixteenth birthday. If the television version of reality is used by our children as a basis for their judgements of the material world, we have cause for concern. If they use television images to judge other people, we are in deep trouble, given the power and importance the television world confers on certain categories of people and the way in which it denies them to others.

TV presents the child with a distorted definition of reality. The child in the affluent suburb or the small midwestern town exists within his own limited reality. His experience with social problems or people of different races, religions, or nationalitites is limited. To the extent that television exposes him to a diversity of people and ideas, it surely expands the boundaries of this reality. It is precisely because he now relies so heavily on TV to define other realities for him that we must examine so carefully what those images are. If they are distorted, inaccurate, or unfair, then television's reality is potentially harmful.

TV says, in effect: This is the way the world works. These are the rules. The images presented on TV tend to be exaggerated or glorified, and so believed and accepted as models to be copied. One demonstration of television's power to influence behavior became apparent during Evel Knievel's heavily promoted attempt to 'fly' his motorcycle over the Snake River. Many children imitated his stunts with their bicycles on home-made ramps, and many landed in hospitals. Even children  who did not see Evel Knievel took up the bike jumping because they caught the idea from friends who had been watching the televised event.

Not only children, but adults too, are enticed into believing that what they see on television is what they'll get in real life. In fact, it can be said with some degree of certainty that all of daytime television as well as nighttime entertainment and news are based on an intense effort, more often than not successful, by the people who produce television programs to make the viewers believe that it is a real picture of life. If this were not the case, the bottom line of television—advertising—would not be nearly so costly, or so profitable. The fatal fallacy in the industry position (that people know they are watching make-believe and therefore will not be induced to act in the ways the characters act on the screen) is that it is totally inconsistent with the television business. **It hardly makes sense to claim that for five minutes people will, while watching make-believe characters in a drama, resolutely put the thought of any imitation out of mind, and switch gears in a second in order to emulate other characters recommending a toilet tissue, detergent, automobile, or beer. Then, after the commercial plug, once again switch back to make-believe. Indeed, it is precisely the validity of the claim that viewers will imitate the characters they see in commercials on which rests the entire financial empire of television.** The reason that networks are so successful in selling commercial time for the vast amounts of money that they do is because they know that a large portion of the viewing audience will believe the "reality" of what they see and be persuaded to purchase the advertised products.

Image of the Thing

"All of society is slipping into a greater reliance on the image of the thing rather than the real thing itself. Television is no better or worse than the rest of society, but it is the major instrument by which, at present, we hasten the process of alienation in our young and interfere with the processes of ego strengthening which grow primarily through contact with reality, not images, through anticipation and interaction with people and things, not through passivity and imitation," quotes Wilkins.[2]

It isn't only children who are affected by television. Studies show that adolescents and adults, too, are influenced by what they watch on TV. For many, **television is used as an escape from the stress of everyday life. Weary homemakers take a break from their busy schedules to watch their favorite daytime serial. The characters on the soaps are entertaining and many men as well as women find it both fun and stimulating to experience "life" (unreal though it may be) vicariously through these fictional friends.** In the United States, television has become the major form of relaxation after a hard day at the office. This isn't so, as was proven by Roderic Gorney. This group found that television viewing could heighten tension and aggression rather than lessen it. In this study, 183 couples living in Los Angeles were asked to watch specific programs. The shows were divided into four categories: heavily violent, helful programs, light entertainment, and a mixture of all three. The men were told to choose shows from only one category and watch them exclusively for a week. Meanwhile, the women were secretly monitoring their husbands' behavior. Results indicated changes in behavior as a consequence of television viewing. Those who watched helpful programs showed a marked decrease in the amount of harmful behavior and aggressive moods exhibited. They were willing to play with their children or help them with homework. Men who watched violent shows remained much the same or became more aggressive. They were likely to start an argument or kick a child's toy left behind on the living room floor.[3]

The Video Tutor

What does the child learn from his video tutor? Carol Kimmel, past president of the National Congress of Parents and Teachers, contends that **what television principally offers children "is a training ground for guerilla warfare."**[4] Over the span of a week, children can be presented with demonstrations of how to kill or maim other human beings and animals that range from the prosaic (guns, knives, bludgeons, poisons, electricity, gas, garrotes, hatchets, drownings) to the more exotic (bee venom, boomerangs, spears, maces, spike heels). They are shown from time to time how to make and handle firearms, molotov-coctails and other grisly weapons, and often given justification for their use. Dr. Richard E. Palmer, former president of the American Medical Association adds that television violence is both a mental health problem and an environmental issue. "In my opinion," says Palmer, "television may be creating a more serious problem than air pollution."[5]

Kung Fu Causes Trouble For Teachers

The "world" according to TV and the real world are two quite different places. What TV tells us about violence, sexuality, material goods, and human beings influences our feelings, behaviors, and judgements before we are taught by life experience.

Television programming tends to present cues upon which the frustrated viewer can pattern his aggressive behavior. Muriel Broadman tells this story: "Teachers have told me that at one time they dreaded Fridays. This was because on Thursday

night ABC-TV aired a program called "Kung Fu," starring David Carradine. Although the premise of the program was that violence is abhorrent to a sentient being, all its problems were eventually solved by the hero's (reluctantly) hurling his opponent into unconsciousness, breaking his bones or performing some similar little act to point out the error of his ways. All the next day in school the children, boys and girls alike, were difficult to control. Not only in the playground and hallways but also in the classroom scraps erupted at every turn. The children kicked at each other, mostly in play, but not always. Discipline was exhausting to maintain. The familiar expression 'Thank God it's Friday' had ironic implications for teachers as long as "Kung Fu" kept its Thursday time slot. Children's play reflects their interests, and play deals more and more with imitating favorite TV shows."[6]

Television has been blamed for bad marriages, divorces, and even murder.

Did TV Make Him Do It?

During a two week period in October 1977, TV violence was codefendent in a murder trial. On June 4, 1977, Ronald Zamora, 15, killed his next door neighbor Elinor Haggart, a Miami Beach widow. Zamora and a friend were in the process of burglarizing the home of the 82 year-old woman. Finding the boys in the midst of their burglary, Mrs. Haggart warned them that she was going to call the police, whereupon Zamora shot her to death. Four days later, Zamora confessed to the murder and four months later went to trial for charges of first degree murder, burglary, robbery, and possession of a firearm while committing a felony.

Zamora's defense attorney, Ellis Rubin, pleaded that his client was temporarily insane at the time of the murder because he was "suffering from and acted under the influence of prolonged, intense involuntary, subliminal television intoxication."

95

Zamora's parents described their son as a "TV addict" who watched six hours daily and favored cops-and-robbers programs such as *Kojak, Baretta,* and *Starsky and Hutch.* Kojak was his idol, and Zamora's parents testified that the boy went as far as to ask his father to shave his head so he would look more like his hero. A psychiatrist, Dr. Michael Gilbert, examined the boy and testified that Zamora had compared the situation to an episode of Kojak: He recalled some program where a woman who had been shot got up and walked away, and he said he felt that might happen. Dr. Gilbert further asserted that Zamora's shooting Mrs. Haggart when she threatened to call the police was a "conditional response" similar to that of a dog who automatically responds to a bell to get his meals. In Gilbert's words, "The woman's statement 'I'm going to call the police' was a symbol of everything Zamora had seen on television and he reacted to rub out the squealer." This was claimed to be the result of Zamora's addiction to television and his long years of watching crime shows and horror movies.

Rubin labeled television an "accessory to the crime" throughout the trial and stated: "It is inevitable that TV will be a defendant. I intend to put television on trial." In his closing remarks, Rubin said, "If you and I can be influenced by short commercials to buy products, certainly an hour 'commercial' on murder could influence this boy when he's seen them over and over."

Testimony by other psychiatrists and psychologists challenged Gilbert's testimony and Rubin's defense claims. Several mental health officials rejected the conditioned response theory and the temporary insanity plea. After nearly two weeks of testimony, the jury deliberated for less than two hours and found Ronald Zamora guilty of murder, burglary, armed robbery, and possession of a firearm. The verdict resulted in Zamora facing an automatic life sentence with chance for parole after 25 years. Apparently, the state had not sought the death penalty because of Zamora's age. *Note: Ronald Zamora, who was serving his life sentence, filed a $25 million lawsuit against all three commercial networks claiming they were responsible for his murdering his neighbor in 1975.*[7]

By no means are we saying that all of television is harmful. There is some wonderful programming available—first class drama, ballet, concerts, opera, theater presentations, not to mention religious programs, can be seen by the discerning viewer—such as "once in a lifetime" events: the wedding of a prince, activities in the space program, or the Olympics can be educational and enjoyable. Every year the National PTA organization publishes a list of recommended commercial network programs that make a positive contribution to the quality of family life. The important thing that we as parents, spouses, and consumers must remember is that the world of television generates a profound and lasting influence on our lives. The awesome task of controlling TV viewing, admittedly, is a difficult one.

9

The Experts Speak

"Our pictures are absolutely clean. The monster might abduct the young bride, but only to kill her," **a producer of horror films—some watched by** **children on television—said with a touch of pride.** It is ironic what we tolerate on television. Imagine driving past your local shopping center and finding that someone has built a scaffold on the roof. After discussing it with your neighbors, you learn that store employees plan to stage a hanging every hour on the hour to draw large crowds to their shopping center. But don't worry. They aren't using real people, simply actors. Another shopping center, learning of the first one's success, decides to stage a rape every fifteen minutes. Again you need not worry, for the participants will be well-paid actors and actresses. We would, of course, be outraged by such actions, yet we accept them as perfectly normal on television.[1]

The American child is learning how to commit crime, inflict pain, and generally ignore the needs of others, thanks to TV. Exposure to violent scenes on television and in the movies is a key factor in stimulating youth violence, reported U.S. Surgeon General C. Everett Koop in 1982. Nearly 75 percent of all prime-time network drama contains some act of physical, mental, or verbal violence, with an average of more than seven violent acts per hour on late evening programming. Nearly half of all characters on prime-time television participate in some violence, about one tenth in killing. A prime-time study done in

1983 by the Media Institute found an average of 1.7 overwhelmingly violent crimes per show programmed on ABC, CBS and NBC. The National Institute of Mental Health found a similar connection, and added the fact that children's weekend programming carries an average of eighteen violent acts per hour. By the time young people reach the age of eighteen, they could have witnessed some eighteen thousand murders.[2]

Early Research

The effect of television violence has been a hotly debated issue for more than three decades. As public concern about violence mounted, psychologists developed theories of how this material might influence young viewers. Early inquiries are important because they laid the foundation for later work by defining the issues and setting forth the basic theories of exactly how TV violence might work its effects.

"It is clear that television, whose impact on the public mind is equal to or greater than that of any other medium is a factor in molding the character, attitudes and behavior patterns of America's young people," reported the Senate Subcommittee on Juvenile Delinquency in 1964.[3]

Hearings on the role of the mass media in 1969 concluded that: "There is sufficient evidence that mass media presentations, especially portrayals of violence, have negative effects upon audiences . . . We believe it is reasonable to conclude that a constant diet of violent behavior on television has an adverse effect on human character and attitudes. Violence on television encourages violent forms of behavior, and fosters moral and social values about violence in daily life which are unacceptable in a civilized society . . . Television is emphasizing violent, antisocial styles of life."[4] These finding were expanded in the Surgeon General's report of 1969.

Surgeon General's Report

Social scientists and communications researchers have conducted more than fifty separate studies of media violence involving more than ten thosand children from all types of social backgrounds. The Surgeon General's Scientific Advisory Committee on Television and Social Behavior funded many of the studies. Congress commissioned this panel, in 1969 to determine scientifically the effects of violence upon its viewers. Researchers consistently found some significant relationship between TV violence and aggressive or other objectionable behavior by children and adolescents. These attempts to demonstrate a direct causal relationship between viewing of actual violent TV content and many measures of a child's willingness to hurt other children resulted in the following conclusions:

1. The more the child or adolescent watches violent television programming, the more aggressive he is likely to be.
2. Aggressiveness leads to a preference for violent television programs.
3. Television encourages violence in adolescents who are already high in aggression.
4. Continued exposure to violence causes the average child to accept aggression as a mode of behavior.
5. Aggressive habits are built over time by exposure to aggressive TV content.
6. Those children who viewed a violent television program were less likely to report violence in a stereoscopic image than those who viewed a nonviolent program, suggesting that they had become at least temporarily less sensitive to it.

Sufficient controversy surrounded publication of the Surgeon General's Report to warrant follow-up hearings and more research into the effects of TV and film violence.

Power and Rewards

Since most television programs showed aggression as a good technique for power and achievement, investigations about this theory were conducted. In one such study, Bandura, Ross and Ross exposed a group of nursery school boys and girls to a television program in which one character, Johnny, refused another, Rocky, the opportunity to play with some toys. The program goes on to show a series of aggressive responses by Rocky, including hitting Johnny with a rubber ball, shooting darts at Johnny's cars, hitting Johnny with a baton, lassoing him with a hula-hoop, and so on. At the end of this sequence, Rocky (the aggressor) is playing with all of Johnny's toys, treating himself to sweet beverages and cookies, and finally departs with Johnny's hobby horse

under his arm and a sack of Johnny's toys over his shoulder. At this point, a commentator announces that Rocky was victorious. For a second group, the program was rearranged so that after Rocky's initial aggression, Johnny retaliated by administering a sound thrashing to him. Two other groups served as controls; in one, a nonaggressive television program was observed, and in the second no television program was seen. The children were then observed while playing in a special test room. The results showed clearly that those who saw a rewarded aggressor showed far more aggression themselves than children in the other groups. At the conclusion of the experiment the children were asked to state which of the characters, Rocky or Johnny, they would prefer to imitate. 60 percent of those who observed Rocky rewarded for his behavior indicated that they would select him as a model. Only 20 percent of those who saw him punished indicated that they would choose to emulate him. Additionally, the authors noted an example of how modeled aggressive acts may influence children. One of the girls who expressed disapproval of Rocky's behavior as it occurred, later displayed many of his aggressive actions.[5]

The Aggression Machine

A number of early studies employed a method that measured how much a person was willing to inflict pain on others. Originally devised by psychologist Arnold Buss and referred to as "the aggression machine," the method involved having participants think that they were giving another person electric shocks. (No real shocks were given—the person hooked to the machine was a researcher.) For example, in one version participants were told that the effects of punishment on learning were being tested and that they would serve in the role of "teacher." The participant was free to choose how strong of a shock given for each wrong answer by the "learner." Thus shock intensity becomes the measure of interest. In one early study using the aggression machine, hospital attendants, high school boys, and young women viewed either the knife-fight scene from *Rebel With A Cause* or a film of adolescents engaging in constructive activities. Both before and after viewing the film, everyone participated in an experiment which supposedly required shocking another person for making errors on a learning test. The critical measure was the difference in the intensity of the shocks given during the two sessions. In all three groups, those who saw the aggressive film gave stronger shocks in the second session that did those who saw the constructive film.

The aggression machine was subsequently used in many other investigations which demonstrated both that viewing violence increases aggression and that laboratory shock is related to real life violence.

Network Sponsored Research

The network undertook research of their own to evaluate the claim that TV violence resulted in aggressive behavior. CBS sponsored two major studies. In 1973 Milgram and Shotland focused on the antisocial act of stealing from a charity donation box. This was a unique experiment in that CBS actually produced the experimental programs. Three versions of a *Medical Center* episode

were produced which modeled stealing in varying ways. The overall plot revolved around Tom, an orderly at the hospital, who had been laid off just when his wife needed a major operation. His hardship occurred at the time that the hospital was conducting a charity drive. In the key scene, Tom was alone in a room with a large plastic container for cash contributions into which the public had placed lots of money—visible money. As the disconsolate man looked at the container, the camera showed the audience that the container was

104

broken. One could easily reach in and scoop out the money. One version showed Tom stealing the money and consequently going to jail for it. In a second version, he stole the money and got away with it. In the third version he was shown being tempted to steal the money, then donating a coin. Audiences were shown one of the *Medical Center* episodes in a theater. In each experiment, several hundred participants ranging in age from high school seniors to a mixed sample of adults, were offered a free radio to view the show. They were told that the research was to judge commercials and the radio could be picked up one week later at another location. The situation was designed to be a frustrating one. When participants arrived at the location where they were to get their gift, they found only an empty office and a sign indicating that there were no more radios. In the room was a charity box containing coins, a $10 bill, and several $1 bills, one of which was protruding from the box. Concealed cameras recorded the subject's behavior. Hence, a situation was created which was very similar to the TV program.

Milgram and Shotland found that overall there were amounts of money taken, but the stealing that occured did not vary significantly with the episode version shown. Some participants, however, lost their temper and damaged the room.

Justification

In real life, it is considered more appropriate to act aggressively when one is justified than when one is not. Therefore, whether or not the violence seen on television or in a movie sequence was justified had to be considered. The reason for thinking that justification would be an important factor is clear. In an experiment by Berkowitz, a group of college students was insulted by a researcher then shown a film exhibiting either justified or unjustified aggression. Finally, they were given a chance to shock the one who had insulted them. The young men who were most likely to give a large number of longer duration shocks were also those who had been angered and then shown entertainment in which aggression with good cause was depicted. Later investigations examined some of the factors that influence justification. Some college men were angered, not by insulting them, but by having an experimenter give them a large number of electric shocks in a learning experiment. The men saw one version of the knife-fight scene from *Rebel Without A Cause*. In one condition, the violence was caused by revenge, in another self-defense, in a third those two were combined, and in one no justification was provided at all. The students then had the oppotunity to shock their aggressor. Students in the group that saw a combination of vengence and self-defense gave more and longer shocks to the experimenter. Berkowitz and Geen predicted that a violent film would be most likely to trigger aggression when the observers were angry and the available target for their own aggression was in some way related to the violent film.

Punishment

Brodbeck found that children's levels of aggression rose markedly after viewing a cartoon in which the villain was not punished. It appears that youngsters expect aggressive acts to be punished. When they are not, children behave as if they had seen the model rewarded. Also, another researcher found that when a commercial was inserted between the violent act and the consequences, the punishment had no effect.[6]

Researchers at Stanford University not only confirmed the cause-effect relationship between TV violence and aggressive behavior but also documented the similarity between aggressive acts shown on television and those committed by children. Nearly 90 percent of the nursery-school children in the experiment modeled the aggressive behavior of the television character when someone took a favorite toy away from them. These same researchers rewarded or punished aggressive models to determine what effect it had upon preschoolers. Aggressive scores of the children who saw the model rewarded were significantly higher than those of the children who saw the model punished. Comparing their findings, they concluded, "Children have opportunities to observe many episodes in which antisocially aggressive behavior has paid off abundantly, and considering the immediate rewards are much more influential than delayed punishment in regulating behavior, the terminal punishment of the villain may have a weak inhibitory effect on the viewer."[7]

The Conclusions

In short, studies that have employed the most direct measures of violence viewing find correlations between such viewing and various measures of aggressiveness. They hold for both sexes, for children of different ages and from different communities. Researchers have identified these consequences of televised violence upon children:

1. Television violence tends to increase subsequent acts of aggression among children, particularly those who are frustrated.
2. Males and females are equally likely to be influenced by exposure.
3. Children between the ages of 8 and 12 are more likely to be affected than are either older or younger youth.
4. Children tend to copy aggressive behavior shown on television.
5. Television teaches children that violence is a justified and acceptable means of resolving conflict.
6. Television tends to distort a child's perceptions of reality.
7. Television violence tends to make children less sensitive to violence in general.

Our conclusion is that TV and other media violence can arouse children and youth, instigate copying of aggressive and antisocial acts, and shape the values of the young regarding a variety of undesirable and antisocial behaviors.

World-Wide Parallels

A unique investigation of aggressive behavior in childen was carried out in Australia, Finland, Israel, Poland, and the United States between 1977 and 1983. The aims of the investigation were to establish the generality of a relation between viewing of television violence and the occurrence of violent behavior. Huesmann and Eron simultaneously studied children from several countries that have different rates of crime and vary in availability of television. They wanted to discover the role that a child's exposure to violence plays in teaching him or her aggressive acts. Because violence appears on television to a much larger extent than in real life, the TV provides more opportunities to experience violence than real life does.

In the selected countries, the United States has 3 to 10 times more homicides. Statistics also show that the United States has over one and one half times more TV sets than any other country and almost three times the number of programming hours. Huesmann and Eron examined a television guide for one representative week during the study in each country and counted the number of programs shown that contained explicit scenes of interpersonal violence. This data indicates that television usage and exposure to scenes of violence vary substantially across the countries. Absolute exposure to TV violence is by far the highest in the United States, although the percentage of programming hours devoted to violence is remarkably similar in all of the countries. Also, it should be noted that violent shows from the United States frequently constitute a large portion of the violence broadcast in other countries, because we export TV shows to them.

"The aggressiveness of a child is determined most by the extent to which a child's environment frustrates and victimizes the child, provides aggressive models, and reinforces aggression."[8] Huesmann believes that social behavior is controlled largely by programs for behavior (scripts) that a child acquires during a sensitive period in his or her development. Faced with a social problem, the child searches his memory for an appropriate script for behaving. Aggressive scripts are learned by observing others' behaviors, therefore media violence provides examples of violence from which aggressive scripts can be learned.

On the whole, the results of this study were consistent in all countries and consistent with results of other similar investigations. More aggressive children watch more violence in the media in almost every country.

Agression in American Children

The United States leads the world in violent programming with about 188 hours per week.[9] Depending on the country, TV violence viewing coupled with identification with actors best predicted tendencies toward aggression. In the United States, early aggression significantly predicted increases in later violence viewing for boys and girls.

In this study over 700 American children, their parents and friends were interviewed between 1977 and 1980. They were asked about their TV viewing habits, their aggressiveness, and their psychosocial environment.

Two approaches were employed in measuring the aggressive behavior —peer nominations and self-ratings.

An aggression score was comuted by asking each child in the class to list all other children in the class who engage in 10 specific aggressive behaviors. All 10 items fit the definition of aggression as "which injures or irritates another person:"

1. does not obey the teacher
2. often says "give me that"
3. gives dirty looks or sticks out their tongue at other children
4. makes up stories and lies to get other children into trouble
5. does things that bother others
6. starts a fight over nothing
7. pushes or shoves children
8. is always getting into trouble
9. says mean things
10. takes other children's things without asking[10]

The Rogers Adjustment Inventory was used to encourage youngsters to give candid self-evaluations by rating their own similarity to fictional children (e.g. "John runs faster than anyone in his class. Am I just like John, a little bit like John, or not at all like John?") Four aggressive behaviors similar to ones in the peer-nomination index were presented in this format. The results of the interviews:

1. Average TV violence viewing in the U.S. peaked in the third grade.

2. The children who watched the most television violence were the most aggressive in all grades.

3. Females were less affected by violence viewing than were males.

4. Children's scripts for social behavior are learned at a very early age and are resistant to change.

5. The relation between violence viewing and aggression seems to depend strongly on the regularity of exposure. Watching mild violence regularly is more likely to cause aggressive acts than is occasional viewing of severe violence.

6. The more a child identifies with the actors who are aggressors or victims, the more likely is the child to be influenced by the scene, believing the behaviors to be appropriate and expected. Boy's and girl's aggressiveness relate about equally strongly to male and female actor violence.

7. Children's perception of television violence as realistic declined significantly with age, but remained substantial in every grade.

8. Television violence can affect a child, regardless of his or her initial level of aggression.

9. Unpopularity led to an increase in TV diet of more violence over the 2 years, but television violence viewing did not lead to a decrease in popularity.

10. Children who were aggressive or watched a lot of violent television tended to get lower grades in school.

In conclusion, at certain periods in a child's development (ages 6-11) extensive exposure to television violence promotes aggressive behavior on the part of the child. Aggressive habits that are established during this time are resistant to change and often persist into adulthood. Children who have poor academic skills behave more aggressively, watch more TV violence, and believe that the violent programs they watch are showing life as it really is. A child who is constantly exposed to violence is more likely to develop aggressive solutions to social problems. The relation between TV habits and aggression is not limited to countries with large amounts of programming and is not limited to boys.

The following pages
show "movie and video posters"
popular with many of today's youth.

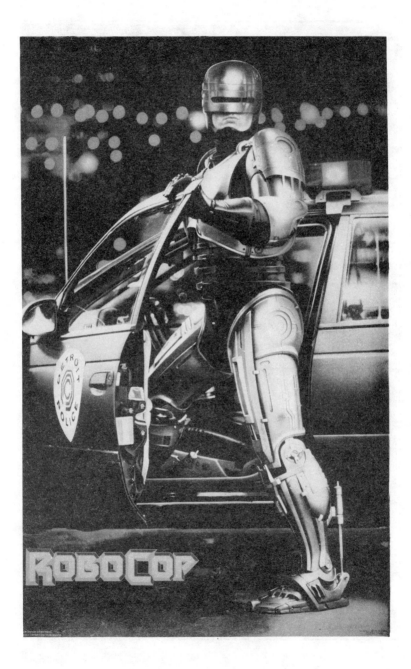

CURRENTLY IN THEATRICAL RELEASE
UNTAMED
UNCAGED
UNLEASHED
IN SPACE
STAR SLAMMER
THE ESCAPE
JACK H. HARRIS PRESENTS a FRED OLEN RAY FILM
Starring ROSS HAGEN SANDY BROOKE SUSAN STOKEY MARYA GANT DAWN WILDSMITH
Special appearances by ALDO RAY and JOHN CARRADINE
Produced by JACK H. HARRIS and FRED OLEN RAY Screenplay by MICHAEL D. SONYE
Music by ANTHONY HARRIS Directed by FRED OLEN RAY
WORLDWIDE ENTERTAINMENT CORP. PICTURES
VIDMARK
ENTERTAINMENT
A VIDMARK Release
Artwork and Design ©1988 VIDMARK
Printed in U.S.A.
R
RESTRICTED

A vengeance-crazed
hunter searching
for his daughter...

Five youths
stalking an
inhuman mutation...

They have just
stepped into the
alien-spawned
realm of
Demonwarp...
and a wave of
unearthly terror
is about to begin!

Enter a prime-evil world of future shock and alien terror.

DEMONWARP

A transmutation into terror

VIDMARK ENTERTAINMENT in association with DESIGN PROJECTS INCORPORATED   Presents "DEMONWARP"
Starring GEORGE KENNEDY   DAVID MICHAEL O'NEILL   PAMELA GILBERT
BILLY JACOBY   COLLEEN McDERMOTT   HANK STRATTON   Co-Starring JOHN DURBIN   JOE PRAML
Director of Photography R. MICHAEL STRINGER   Edited by W. PETER MILLER   Music by DAN SLIDER
Story by JOHN BUECHLER   Screenplay by JIM BERTGES & BRUCE AKIYAMA   Executive Producer MARK AMIN
Produced by RICHARD L. ALBERT   Directed by EMMETT ALSTON

VIDMARK
ENTERTAINMENT

THEY TAKE NO PRISONERS, THEY SHOW NO MERCY.

COMMANDO SQUAD

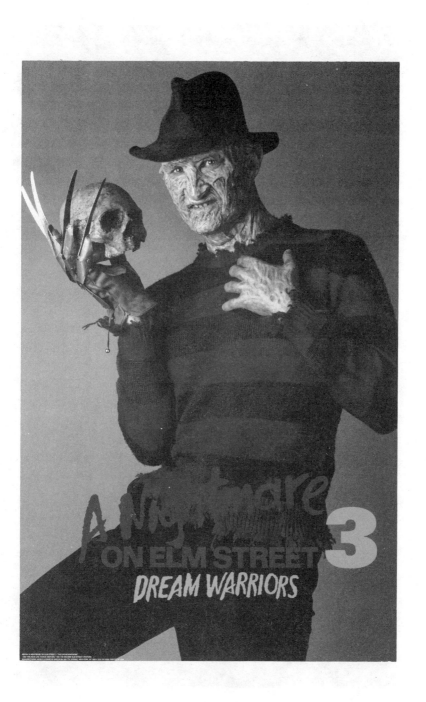

A Nightmare
ON ELM STREET 3
DREAM WARRIORS

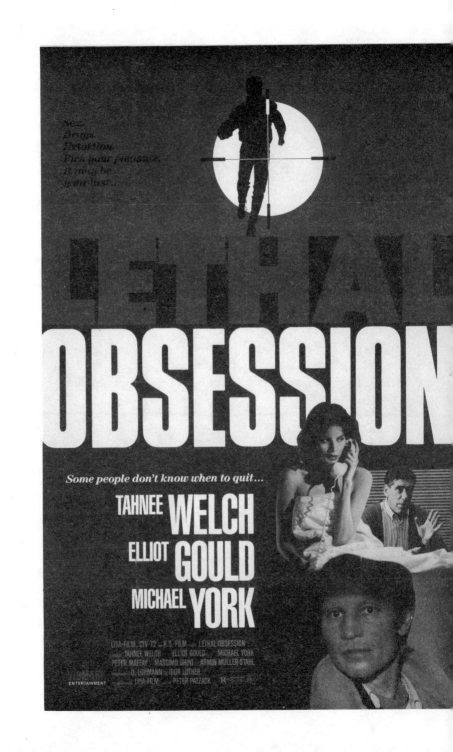

10

Consider The Commercials

"My bologna has a first name. It's O-S-C-A-R. My bologna has a second name. It's M-A-Y-E-R. I love to eat it everyday, and if you ask me why, I'll say, 'cause Oscar Mayer has a way with B-O-L-O-G-N-A."

How many other jingles or catchy phrases from television commercials can you think of? Children seldom go away from the TV without humming a tune, chanting a phrase, or suffering from the "I wants" triggered by one of the numerous advertisements that they saw during their favorite programs. It is impossible for them not to be influenced by these fast paced, technicolor, bits of fancy camera work. Do you have trouble deciding whether you want dish detergent that enables you to see your reflection in the plates, one that takes grease out of your way, or the brand that has longer-lasting suds? It is no wonder that children who enter grocery and department stores smiling inevitably have tears running down their cheeks before long, and parents find themselves harried and frustrated as a direct result of dealing with the effects of commercial advertising.

We weren't surprised when we recently read that **a group of 400 children were given fifteen minutes to list all the products they could remember from TV commercials. Some were able to write down as many as fifty, including fifteen different brands of beer. Almost all of the brand names were spelled correctly.**[1]

Knowing children's vulnerabilities, advertisers spend about $700 million yearly pitching products at them. Advertising strategists know from their sophisticated research that children will learn efficiently from television and will easily become the advertiser's representative in the home. The typical child in America sees roughly 400 TV advertisements per week that tell him what to like, what to want, what to do, and what to beg for. Long before the TV child can make purchases by himself, he will influence the consuming behavior of adults.[2]

Parents in the United States tend to fear the teaching potential of commercials. Because advertisers have perfected their techniques, this fear is justified. Children learn from commercials. They remember slogans, jingles, and brand names. They often try to influence their parents to buy advertised goods. Children below age seven or so are particularly vulnerable to such effects, probably because they do not discriminate between the program and the commercial and do not realize that the purpose of commercials is to sell goods; they simply accept commercials as presenting information like any other television format. It is because advertising is teaching us and our children that we need to take a closer look at exactly how this facet of the media is influencing us.

How Advertising Affects Taste and Preference

Advertisers are reliant on symbols. They use certain symbols to summon images or feelings that an audience can identify with. They use symbols so that the consumer will make an association between the symbol used and the advertiser's product. Patriotic symbols are good examples of this and are quite effective. By using bands and parades, picnics, ball games and patriotic music, advertisers hope to arouse a strong sentiment in the viewer that he will transfer to the product.

Religious and revered or ancient symbols are also heavily used. Lighting angles show products in almost heavenly lights. Consider the grape commercial showing Adam and Eve in paradise, featuring grapes as the heavenly alternative to the apple. The grapes are illuminated, and celestial voices ring out. Another commercial for toilet paper shows babies pictured as little cherubs wearing wings. The message is that the product is divinely superior to the product of its competitor.

The influence of the advertiser does not end with the commercial. Advertisers pay for their products to be displayed in the most flattering context. Car companies don't want to sponsor a drama about a car wreck. Food advertisers are guaranteed that their products will not be shown back to back with a toilet cleaning commercial, or a commercial for an antacid or deodorant.

In addition to influencing the public's taste within the commercial and without, advertisers also control what programs are seen on the air. The TV business is so lucrative, that often programs can't afford to be different or pioneering, because there may not be anyone to sponsor them. Advertisers like to sponsor shows that will appeal to the broadest of tastes and to the group of Americans who have the most buying power.

You may be wondering what this has to do with the topic of this book, *Horror and Violence*. We authors simply want to stress to you the powerful message that advertisers are sending into our homes. The products themselves have been dealt with in *Turmoil In The Toy Box*. Here we want to concentrate on the message, and the fact that many advertisers seem to think that using violence in their printed ads and television commercials is the accepted, if not better way to sell products to the American public.

Effects of Violence in TV Commercials

The National Association of Broadcasters code prohibits the portrayal of violent, antisocial, or unsafe acts in commercials. The NAB code (1976) states: "Material shall not be used which can reasonably be expected to frighten children or provoke anxiety, nor shall material be used which contains a portrayal of or appeal to violent, dangerous, or otherwise antisocial behavior.

"Advertisements and products advertised shall be consistent with generally recognized standards of safety. Advertisements shall not include demonstrations of any product in a manner that encourages harmful use or dramatizations of actions inconsistent with generally recognized standards of safety."[3]

Despite these guidelines, Schuetz and Sprafkin (1979) found 133 aggressive acts in a single Saturday morning sample of 414 commercials. The amount of aggression in the commercials was about three times that found in the programs surrounding them. Further, there was the greatest concentration of aggressive acts in cereal commercials. Presumably, these elements were included to capture the attention of the young viewer.

Due to a problem with definition and the subjective nature of the decision about safety, it is more difficult to determine the incidence of unsafe acts in commercials.

Poulos (1975) examined a series of cereal commercials which showed an adult picking wild berries or a part of a pine tree, noting that the vegetation was good to eat and in some cases adding some to his cereal bowl. The Federal Trade Commission had received several complaints from parents who were concerned about the demonstration of eating wild vegetation. Children between 5 and 11 years-old were asked to judge whether a series of familiar and unfamiliar plants was good or bad to eat. They were shown the commercials, then tested again. While the broadcast did not change the youngsters' judgements about familiar plants, it did produce a more accepting attitude toward the unfamiliar plants, especially those most similar in appearance to those in the advertisement. The results, therefore, suggested that after viewing these commercials, children would be more inclined to eat potentially harmful wild vegetation. The cereal company withdrew this series of commercials.[4]

Similarly, while Spiderman and various cartoon characters talked about delicious multi-flavored ("I like the cherry best") chewable vitamins and "new superhero vitamins," numerous children were reported hospitalized for overdoses.

Violence in Children's Advertising

What would your guess be as to the percentage of the ads in children's programming that are for food, primarily sugar-coated cereals, cookies, candies, and soft drinks? If you guessed over 50 percent, you are correct, and the other 50 percent? That one isn't difficult either—toys.

No one can sit down and watch any half-hour of cartoons or prime-time program targeted for children without being shown at least a dozen toys that you not only deserve, but NEED to feel good and have a pleasant life.

The problem is that more and more of the toys are war or violence-oriented and the commercials show the children how to play aggressively with them. "The only place where violence on kids' TV doesn't seem utterly antiseptic [too clean] is in ads for the action-adventure toys on which the shows are based," says Todd Gitlin, associate professor of sociology and director of the mass communications program at the University of California. "Only there do we sense real aggression, some actual human venom at work. A few years ago, these commercials were little films about kids playing with their toys, now they are tiny ritual outdoor battles among three or four usually white, mostly blonde boys (never a girl) in vaguely suburban settings. Each holds a Transformer or a Go-Bot or a He-Man figure on a stage of uneven rocks. Grimacing and growling, the boys insult each other's figures, exchange oaths and curses ('Next bash is on you, bone-face!') while parading their toys, often to the crushing drumbeat of Japanese-style background chants for the product. Only here, in the ads, can you actually feel the urge to smash, insult, destroy—all connected to the urge to rush out and buy."[5]

The latest in children's programming is *interactive toys*. These toys are explained further in Chapter Ten. Basically, these toys are made to be used in conjunction with a cartoon program. The commercials tell children to purchase special military weapons that they can use to shoot the "bad guys" on the television screen during the program. A score is recorded for the child to keep track of his "kill."

Ads for violent toys made by Tyco (Military construction toys), Fisher Price (Military Construx), Lego (Blacktron Renegade Attack Jet Fighter), Mattel (Mad Scientist and Captain Power war toys, Soldier of the Future Jet Fighter) as well as Laser Tag, G. I. Joe and many others can be found in *Good Housekeeping, 3-2-1-Contact,* and *Better Homes and Gardens. Boys' Life* regularly offers martial arts fighting stars and various knives.

The promoting of war and killing to children as patriotic and exciting is misguided. **Giving a gun to a doll doesn't turn it into a boy's doll, it turns it into a violent doll.** Fighting might be normal behavior for some children, but it isn't healthy behavior. Allowing toy companies to sell war as an exciting game for children so that they can maximize their profits is not healthy for our country. Not only does this type of toy encourage violence, but the commercials for them are a lesson in behaving violently. Children are learning the lesson as is evidenced by the following case history:

A 10 year-old Memphis, Tennessee boy shot his 11 year-old friend with a .22 caliber rifle after watching a TV commercial for the Laser Tag game. The 11 year-old is hospitalized in serious condition and may be partially paralyzed. The boys told police they "saw the people on TV shooting each other, so they decided to do like the people on TV were doing." The boys' grandmother and guardian had the gun hidden under her bed.[6]

BBB Protests Mattel War Ads

The children's advertising unit of the Counsel of Better Business Bureaus thinks Mattel's TV commercial and associated program for Captain Power and his military fighter jet XT-7 may be confusing children by blending fantasy and programming with commercialism. Mattel's commercial for this toy was protested. The ad opens with what seems to be a cake commercial that is interrupted by static and voices. Viewers hear, "I think we're getting through, Captain." The Captain replies, "What year?" His aide replies, "19-uh-87—I think. Try it." The ad turns into a 60 second introduction for the Captain Power interactive military war toys line. Captain Power appeals to viewers to fire their military jet XT-7 "invisible beams" at "enemy targets" that threaten "human life." He adds, "The power of the future is in your hands." The BBB questions whether the commercial makes it more difficult for children to distinguish between fantasy and reality. He says the featured toy is misleading to children and the ad could "hamper a young child's ability to distinguish between program/editorial content and advertising," and the ad presents an "urgency of the message" to put "extreme sales pressure" on children who are not "as prepared as adults to make judicious independent purchase decisions."[7]

Mattel isn't the only company who is promoting violence in their advertising. The amount of violence used in children's advertising these days is incredible. The average 4 to 8 year-old will see 1,000 thirty-second and 180 thirty-minute cartoon commercials selling war toys this year. This is the equivalent of 18 days of classroom instruction in pro-war entertainment. Beside the constant promotion of violent toys like G. I. Joe, Star Wars, Transformers, He-Man, Starriors, etc., there is a heavy use of violence in ads for non-violent products.

NCTV sampled 2 hours of Saturday morning TV and found:
1. Marvel toys selling "Secret Wars" war toys.
2. Crest toothpaste showing superheroes shooting down the bad guy's airplane.
3. Indiana Jones take-off selling Wrangler Jeans.
4. A policeman and thief involved in a Cookie Crisp ad.
5. Bubble Yum Gum ad with a tie-in to He-Man toys.
6. Mattel selling a violent Landshark toy as part of the evil Skeletor collection.[8]

When was the last time that you took a serious look at the commercials that interrupt your child's favorite programs? These authors suggest that you take a few minutes next Saturday morning for your own informal survey. You may be surprised at the way your television is teaching your children to play with their toys.

The Supreme Court already has ruled that video games are not a form of speech, and thus not protected by the First Amendment. The same appears true for toys. Controls on advertising are permitted by the U. S. Constitution and the Supreme Court when a compelling interest is involved. Surely, calling a halt to the massive selling of violence to our children is a compelling public interest.

Peek at the Promos

Some of the most hurtful violence, including episodes of wife-beating, child abuse, and drug use, appears before millions of children in the form of program promotions aired during children's typical viewing hours. "Stay up," the child is told during a four o'clock show, "and watch *The Equalizer* hunt down a rapist." (Mommy, what is a rapist?) "See *Magnum P. I.* come to a prostitute's aide." (Daddy, what is a prostitute?) "Follow the Wiseguy as he machine-guns a hit man." (Oh boy, can I stay up?) Of course, these are fictional examples, but if you take a look at the real things—the promos for both prime-time shows and movies—we can guarantee that you'll see worse. Advertisers seem to choose the most violent or sexually explicit scene in the film to lure the viewer. The problem is that these promos are aired during the time when children are sitting with their eyes rivetted to the screen.

A Word About MTV

If MTV is a part of your cable service, do you realize that your child or teenager gets a double-shot of violence? (Some parents don't even know that there are commercials

133

on MTV.) Between videos of questionable merit and some rather unpleasant scenes, there are a few eye-opening commercials.

Iron Maiden rock group advertises its records with a guitar-like axe dripping blood. In an Atari ad a woman is held over a boiling pot about to be cooked alive. Bugle Boy clothing ad features a gun lying on the bed. MTV itself advertises its channel with numerous violent ads, including one with two guitarists using guitars as guns to fire at each other.

Are you certain that you can sleep soundly in the room next to a teen who watches this fare daily?

Prime-Time Commercials

Children are definitely not the only ones to whom the media is selling with violence. Adults are just as vulnerable to the message.

Pirelli Tires is using violence to sell tires on British Television. In the commercial a woman tries to kill her husband by fiddling with the brakes of his car. Expecting her lover to pick her up, her husband arrives instead— her plot foiled by his strong gripping tires.

American International Rent-A-Car is using a boxing format to appeal to businessmen to rent cars. The ad shows president and CEO Nicholas Yabba in a boxing outfit in the ring looking at the reader with the caption, "why this rental company put a fighter in the ring."

British Airways used a TV ad with a woman in chains who is then beheaded because she did not buy British Airways tickets.

Diet Coke uses the violent Remington Steel star Pierce Brosnan for its new ad campaign. In one ad he is being chased by ninja assassins on motorcycles and in jeeps. He cooly says, "Ours is not a perfect world." He spies a waiter inside a passing train serving Diet Coke to a beautiful woman. He jumps onto the side of the train, chased by the ninjas who somersault onto the roof. Looking at the woman drinking Coke through the window he says, "That's why it's so refreshing when you find something really perfect like Diet Coke." The ninjas jump off the train just before it enters a tunnel, and the hero is safe. An earlier advertisement used violence at a middle eastern bar. Brosnan has a dart tossed at him. Hitting a waiter's tray instead, it causes a can of Diet Coke to pour neatly into glasses on the table. Brosnan tosses a piece of ice on the floor and a ninja slips and sails through a window. Diet Coke brand manager states of this campaign, "We're looking for sophistication and adult consumers."[9] This is sophistication? We think not.

Prime-time commercial breaks feature barroom brawls, kung fu exhibitions, Vietnam war atrocities, use of guns, knives and other weapons, and sexual suggestions to send their messages. On top of everything else, networks use film-clips of their most violent scenes as promotional material at station breaks throughout the day. In our opinion, this violence is totally unnecessary and is an insult to the intelligence of a keen viewer. Television sponsors have entirely too much influence on our lives.

The Influence of Sponsors

In 1949 *Man Against Crime* was sponsored by Camel cigarettes. This affected both writing and direction. Mimeographed instructions from the sponsors to the writers not to have "the heavy or any disreputable person smoking a cigarette." They were told not to "associate the smoking of cigarettes with undesirable scenes or situations plot-wise." Cigarettes had to be smoked gracefully, never puffed nervously, and since it might suggest a narcotic effect, "a cigarette was never given to a character to 'calm his nerves.' " No one could cough on *Man Against Crime*, and because there were rumors of an upcoming report on health effects of smoking, nothing was to be done to antagonize doctors.[10]

In the 1950's a change in the power distribution of commercial television eliminated much of the script control of the sponsors, but the advertisers still manage a certain amount of influence. For example, General Motors donated seven Chevrolet Camaros to the long-running series *Mannix* on condition that none would ever be driven by a heavy, and that when two cars crashed, the Chevy would never be the car that got totaled. Chrysler had a similar agreement with the *Mod Squad*. Some sponsor control has bordered on the ridiculous, especially among automobile manufacturers. The Chrysler Building was edited out of a scene of the New York skyline in a program sponsored by a competing car company. "Fording a stream" was deleted from a script for similar reasons. One car manufacturer actually wouldn't allow the name of Abraham Lincoln to be mentioned because Lincoln was a competitive car.

Although our research revealed some of these extreme cases, we were even more surprised to find that a large number of companies advertising on televisiom apparently don't even take the trouble to find out how much violence they are supporting. A class in developmental sociology at the University of Washington monitored network programs and sponsors for a week in February 1974. They determined the sponsors for violent programming, then contacted them for comments. The students discovered that most of the corporations seemed totally and genuinely unaware of the situation. All admitted that they bought commercial time according to audience demographic studies and they paid little attention to program content.[11]

Meredith Baxter-Birney, co-star of NBC's *Family Ties* recently commented, "Television is one of the most potent manipulators on our planet today. How much of our unconscious decision-making process have we given over? This is where we get the message of what's important, what to have and to wear and what to buy." Baxter-Birney sees a lack of reality in television features and commercials alike.

We agree with Ms. Baxter-Birney when she said, "The process of overcoming the illusion created by television must start at home. I don't see television becoming any less a part of our lives, so our obligation is to be alert to the messages that are sent. To educate our children and ourselves against all the pretty people and the pretty situations."[12]

11

Humorous Violence And Cartoons

A beefy figure stands spread-eagled, naked to the waist, wielding a huge axe that is dripping with blood. Two beady eyes look out through a black executioner's mask. A knife as big as a forearm is tucked into the belt loop of his leather pants, its handle resting inches from a bloody tattoo emblazoned on his chest. By his right foot sits a basket filled with dismembered body parts and by his left foot, a human skull. Who is this nasty character? Is he the latest terror-inspiring psychopath in a newly released slasher movie? Is he a demonized worshipper posing for a photojournalist? Is he an image from someone's dreadful, horror-filled nightmare?

The correct answer is none of the above. This macabre figure is known as "Deadly Dudly." He is one of many gruesome animated characters known collectively as the *Garbage Pail Kids*. "Deadly Dudly" and his grotesque companions "Decapitated Hedy," "Dyin' Dinah," and "Brenda Blender" appear on a wildly successful series of bubblegum cards designed not to scare kids, but to humor them. The *Garbage Pail Kids* are just another part of television in the 1980's—the Golden Age of violence in children's toys and television programming.

Due to widespread protests the *Garbage Pail Kids* cannot be seen in their own cartoon series today. CBS

139

was planning a Saturday morning cartoon featuring these maimed and dismembered children, including one who dribbles his head down a basketball court and a black baby impaled with a two-foot diaper pin. However, enough individuals expressed their concern that such levels of sadistic humor did not belong in children's television, and the program was canceled.

Between May of 1985 and the Fall of 1986, 800 million of these cards were sold. The bubblegum cards like many other novelty items and toys became so popular that they were immediately considered for a TV series. After all, such a TV show would have an advance viewership in Garbage Pail Kid card collectors, and the sales of products featured in their own series could be extremely lucrative. Dating back as far as the turn of the century, there has been a close relationship between children's toys and products and the media. This relationship began quite modestly with a popular comic strip character and an enterprising shoe company, but was later turned upside down by a little red-headed doll with freckles.

From Buster Brown to Strawberry Shortcake

In 1904, The Brown Shoe Company purchased the rights to use the name of a popular character from the comic strips, Buster Brown, to promote Brown's line of children's shoes at the World's Fair in St. Louis. With this purchase of Buster Brown, the concept of character licensing was born. As a result of Brown Shoe Company's success with Buster, other companies followed suit. Charlie Chaplin loaned his name to many dolls, books and toys. Later Shirley Temple dolls appeared in stores and Little Orphan Annie turned up on Ovaltine labels. With the advent of TV, merchandisers saw a chance to enhance sales of their toys and products by connecting themselves with popular TV characters.

The old time television merchandising process started with a successful show. Toy companies would pay for the right to make and market a doll of the main character. Then clothing companies would come along and pay for the right to use a popular TV character's picture on pajamas and so on. Popular kiddie TV characters quickly appeared on enormous lines of products for children. Old time merchandising continued to be the most effective style well into the 1970's with the marketing of Sesame Street and Scooby-Doo products spawned from these highly successful shows. In 1977, the nature of children's television and child consumerism changed radically partly because of a young director and entrepreneur named George Lucas. George Lucas established Lucasfilm, a company whose intent was in part to license its own characters, characters soon to be known the world over in a film called *Star Wars*. George Lucas correctly banked on the hope that little plastic figurines of Han Solo, Luke Skywalker and the movie's other characters would become the most sought after toy of that time.

Spurred on by Lucasfilm's success, two employees of the American Greetings Corporation decided to create and license a character who would be instantly popular with young girls. A red-headed girl dressed in pink, dappled with strawberries known as Strawberry Shortcake appeared on the screen. Strawberry Shortcake was designed jointly with the toy group at General Mills and introduced at the 1980 American International Toy Fair in New York by Kenner toys (owned by General Mills). Kenner even produced an animated TV special featuring Strawberry Shortcake. Although the networks rejected the TV special at the time; it wasn't long before Strawberry Shortcake became America's best-loved doll. Because of little Strawberry's success, it occurred to other toy, greeting card, and cereal companies that they too could create and license their own characters. The brilliance of the idea was that the product could *precede* the show. These companies would then make the money formerly made by the TV companies who licensed out popular characters. Not long after producers realized they no longer had to pay for the rights for a licensed character, the broadcasting industry received a tremendous shot in the arm from the Federal Government. Because of Strawberry Shortcake and Uncle Sam, the TV industry would never be the same.

Hello Deregulation, Hello He-Man

In 1981, the broadcasting and toy industries received a boost from the FCC who deregulated the broadcasting industry. TV stations could now air as many commercials as they chose within a given time period. More importantly, this new ruling allowed for the program-length commercial. Any company, wishing to promote sales of a toy or product, could develop a TV series featuring animated versions of its products. The Smurfs and their cartoon show became the first billion dollar money maker for a manufacturer after the deregulation. They were followed by Pac-Man, that "master" of the cartoon universe, He-Man, and a host of others. The end result is that TV has never been more commercialized.

In their wild desires for big, fat profits, manufacturers have never shown less concern for the effects their toys and program-length commercials are having on the well-being of children. Thus we have a major network, CBS, producing a sadistically violent cartoon that features the monstrous Garbage Pail Kid characters, all in the name of the almighty dollar. And that is only part of the story of an industry that has become grotesquely commercial and entirely too violent.

Saturday Morning's Smorgasbord of Violence

Violence is our nation's number one social problem. Aggression may be a natural tendency in human beings; however, violence is a behavior that is learned through observation, imitation and instruction. The first TV generation has matured into the most violent in United States history, committing murder, rape and assault at levels 300 to 600 percent higher than any previous generation.[1]

Violence in cartoons is changing the way that children play. Studies show that there is an increase in hitting, kicking, choking, throwing, holding other children down, pushing, and hurting animals. It is becoming more and more difficult for children to tell the difference between pretend assaults and real ones. Watching violent cartoons can increase selfishness and anxiety in children as well as affect their schoolwork.

The most violent cartoons on the air today are the war cartoons. These can be graphically real, as in *G.I. Joe* or a futuristic fantasy set on a planet light years from earth, such as *He-Man*. **It is easy to discern which war cartoons are the most popular. One doesn't have bother to read broadcasting trade journals or TV magazines. Just go to your local department store and look for the hottest selling toys.**

War Cartoons and War Toys

On the average, most American children see 250 episodes of war cartoons and 800 advertisements for war toys a year. That's roughly equivalent to 22 days of instruction in a classroom intended to teach violence as the only means of resolving conflicts.[2] War cartoons complete with their own line of war toys, continue to appear with each new TV season. No wonder that five of the six top selling toys in the United States are war toys. "Violent toys help rehearse violent behavior," claims expert Dr. Goldstein.[3]

War cartoons average approximately 80 violent acts per hour with an attempted murder every two minutes. Some of the most popular violent cartoons include *G. I. Joe; Transformers; She-Ra, Princess of Power; Thundercats; Voltron; He-Man and the Masters of the Universe; and Captain Power and the Soldiers of the Future.* These cartoons show characters who enjoy repeated attempts to kill each other. Usually the character who is considered *good* is never harmed, whereas the bad guys are routinely killed off. Good or evil, the only recourse that all of these characters use as a means to solving problems is violence. The *Photon* live-action children's program which sells the LJN laser gun, averages an incredible 114 acts of violence per hour, making the thrill of pretending to kill people even more exciting. Sales of the laser gun have skyrocketed.

Besides conveying that negotiation is not an option when dealing with an enemy, war cartoons also assert that war is not real and that weapons do not cause people to die. These programs also suggest that there are no consequences from violence and fighting. Those who argue that war cartoons are not damaging to children say that war has been and always will be a part of life and to shield children from that inevitability is dangerously naive. War is a part of the history of our nation and many nations— that is undeniable. However, the war that our country has known is not the glorified TV version. Should a child be shielded from the realities of war, yet be permitted to watch war cartoons where those on the side of right are never killed? General Sherman, referring to the Civil War, made the same statement that Dwight D. Eisenhower would make years later, "War is hell."

It is our determination that war cartoons that young children see are no crash course in reality. Instead, they clean up war to make it seem like appealing fun.

Joe No Doughboy

At the top of NCTV's list of violent programs is today's G.I. Joe cartoon averaging 84 violent acts per hour. In 1986, G.I. Joe was one of the top three selling toys and continued to be in the top ten throughout 1987. G. I. Joe is very different from the action figure many adults may remember from their childhood. Today's Joe comes with enough equipment to reenact whole action scenarios directly from the TV show. There are a total of 50 figures in the Joe action force and enemy Cobra. Weaponry includes long range artillery machines, tanks, underwater and reconnaissance craft, copters with complete bomb arsenals, a $200 space vehicle launch complex and many more vehicles and weapons.

Of course, since *G.I. Joe* is such a popular TV show, Joe comic books, magazines, lunchboxes, sheets, t-shirts, slippers, and a laser tag game are popular items. Children often feel powerless compared to adults. Watching G.I. Joe, wearing Joe clothes and playing with Joe are ways children can feel powerful. Joe is invincible. Within the series there are always bombings and shootings and fights, but Joe never dies.

Besides glorifying war, the *G.I. Joe* cartoon suggests that people who have foreign accents or who are disabled, disfigured or inhuman should be suspected as enemies. Those are the kinds of individuals that Joe fights in his cartoon. Joe never tries to change or convert his enemy. The only way he deals with them is to fight them or kill them. Cartoon Joe's attitude is best typified by this segment recently seen on the show:

One of the animated heroes beats up a half-dozen terrorists. "Has it ever occurred to you there might be an easier way to settle disputes?" one of the hero's sidekicks asks him. "Yeah," the hero replies. "With a gun."[4]

The prevailing message of G.I. Joe does not suggest that peace is something we like to live with. Another argument against the *G.I. Joe* cartoon and all of his action accessories is that children's play becomes unimaginative. Supplied with all the real-life accessories, children merely mimic what they see on TV, rather than invent their own adventures.

He-Man Still Going Strong

The first cartoon introduced to promote a line of toys from Mattel was *He-Man,* a fantasy developed because marketing research showed that small boys spend one-quarter of their time fantasizing about the forces of good versus the forces of evil. Because their show was rejected by all three major networks. Mattel and Westinghouse decided to distribute *He-Man* in a new way. They syndicated the first 65 episodes to independent stations all over the country. *He-Man* made his debut in 1983, and is the first syndicated cartoon in which every object you can see could be purchased in your local store. Today *He-Man* is the most popular afternoon cartoon in the U.S.

The essential message of *He-Man* is that your enemy is unworthy of respect and must be dealt with through force. He-Man never kills his enemy, although he does destroy evil robots and android type of characters. He-Man's opponents are evil forces that can only be defeated by the "power of Grayskull." The message of He-Man is exactly the opposite of Jesus Christ's message that we try to understand the enemy.

He-Man can be heard to utter the words, "I have the power" every day as his program airs. It was said that after selling 35 million He-Man figures in 1984 (95,628 a day or 66.4 figures every minute) Mattel's salesmen used the pitch, "We have the power."[5] He-Man was so successful with young boys that shortly thereafter, a female

equivalent, She-Ra, was designed for a movie released in 1985. This movie, *She-Ra, Princess of Power,* contained 59 violent acts per hour, including whipping people, flame throwing, gassing the enemy, kidnapping, knocking people out, slavery, using magic spells to control people's minds, paralyzing rays, attempts at mass destruction, and 33 attempted murders.

Many parents do not believe that the *He-Man* series has a negative impact on their children. He-Man is a clean-cut, blonde-haired good leader who has overpowered villains because they were polluting the environment. Occasionally the He-Man cartoons contain prosocial themes, however, they are always obscured in violence.

As with several of these war cartoons, moralistic messages are sometimes tacked on at the end of *He-Man.*

Unfortunately, most kids don't pick up the prosocial message; instead they remember the action and the violence. This has to do in part with the way children watch TV. Many are "flippers," using a remote control to flip back and forth between shows. Younger children are more inclined to see bits and pieces of programs. Even when they do see the whole program, small children cannot organize the scenes or understand the plot or themes in cartoons.

Because the admirable He-Man is so popular with children, they will be even more inclined to imitate his violent, authoritarian style. When violence is performed by good guys it encourages the use of violence as a means of solving problems.

Captain Power and his
Interactive Crimestoppers

Like He-Man, Captain Power and the Soldiers of the Future is the first of its kind in war cartoons for children. Captain Power is an interactive cartoon. Children can purchase toy military weapons to shoot at the TV set while they are watching Captain Power. Computer chips in the gun tell the child whether he has shot the bad guy, or if the bad guy has shot him. **While Captain Power's cartoon is engrossing your child in simulated combat, it is likewise turning your family room into a simulated war zone and your children into Captain Power's crimestoppers.**

This cartoon is the most violent children's program ever produced, according to the International Coalition Against Violent Entertainment (ICAVE). Unlike He-Man, Captain Power is said to kill his enemies on the average of one a minute. The villains on Captain Power, like villains on all the war cartoons, never manage to kill the forces of good.

Concerned about the effects of interactive war cartoons, ICAVE completed studies at their research center in Illinois on 5, 7, and 9 and 10 year-old children. On different days of study, children played with non-violent construction toys or watched the *Captain Power* cartoon (using the interactive toy weapon). On the days the children watched *Captain Power*, they showed increases in playground aggression, exhibiting 81 percent more hitting, kicking, pulling hair, and sitting on top of other children.[6]

Children who purchase the Captain Power weapons can play with the guns without watching the program. They can also watch the TV program without needing a toy gun. However, children are strongly affected by the effects of slick advertising and may feel that they have to have a Captain Power gun to watch the show. So the *Captain Power* cartoon not only reaches new heights in cartoon violence, but also descends to new lows in commercializing children's television.

Money Speaks Louder

The chances that the American viewing public will see voluntary retraction of these war cartoons by broadcasters and producers because of the harmful effects of TV violence are as likely as He-Man being overpowered by a nasty villain. The force of money is strong enough to subdue any occasional twinges of social responsibility. Due to the fact that broadcasters don't have to pay to obtain many of the programs, they make big money off war cartoons. Children's shows are aired in time slots that are not profitable for many other programs. Cartoon producers (often the toy or cereal company) will give the programs for free to broadcasters in exchange for advertising time.

Certain cartoons have gone one step further in attracting networks—just for broadcasting *Thundercats* cartoon, they get 5 percent of all the profits from the toy sales in their area.

Producers do not have to invest a lot of money in assuring a high quality program. After all, their audience is young children—not the most discriminating of viewers. Most of the producers' budget is used for special effects. If you watch these cartoons closely, it appears that little money is appropriated for anything else. Characters are primitively animated and as a result appear very wooden. Voices tend to be monotone. Cartoons with accompanying lines of toys are the most lucrative on TV. Many in the broadcast industry underestimated the money that America would be willing to spend on action figures, weapons, interactive toys and assorted paraphernalia inspired by children's cartoons.

It seems that children and cartoon producers have something in common. Children love adventure. Producers and manufacturers love adventure because adventure means money in today's television market. In their never-ending quest for adventure ideas, long-time animators Hanna-Barbera have turned to the *Bible. The Greatest Adventure Stories from the Bible* are new, animated releases sold primarily through direct mail and religious markets. The first six releases are tales from the Old Testament, including the stories of David and Goliath and Sampson and Delilah. Hanna-Barbera has said The Crucifixion will not be portrayed in their *Bible* animations because it is "too strong for children."[7]

Humorous Violence in TV Programs

Laughter, it has been said is the best medicine. That medicine would be a lot easier to swallow if it weren't laced with the gratuitous violence on humorous cartoons and humorous prime time programs. We laugh when we are comfortable and at ease. When frightened or angry, it is difficult to laugh. Laughing only happens readily when we are willing to make ourselves vulnerable, when our body's defense mechanisms have been turned off.

If we are enjoying a humorous program, and violence erupts in the middle of it, our defenses are down. Subconsciously, we may continue to chuckle through the violence. Eventually, we become more accepting of violence and find it humorous in its own right.

Consider how accepting we are of the violence in *The Three Stooges* program. The Stooges may have been artful comedians, but what kind of message are they conveying to their viewers, who are encouraged to belly laugh at their violent antics? The Associated Press published a national 26 inch article praising the Three Stooges without any mention of the harmful effects of the violence in their shows. The actors are praised for being lovable and aggreeable even though research shows that the show has increased violent behavior in children. Pictures accompanying the article show Curley being choked by two baseball bats and Larry having his eyes poked out.

Other film favorites who appear in shows that are inappropriately violent include *Bugs Bunny* and *Roadrunner, Donald Duck* and *Woody Woodpecker*. The violence in these programs is considered slapstick, yet studies show that slapstick violence has harmful effects on normal children. The NCTV rating system counted 56 violent acts per hour in the *Bugs Bunny/Roadrunner* show. In one episode of a *Donald Duck* cartoon, his nephews hit him in the mouth, sink his boat, tie him to a stake, shoot him, and electrocute him. Even *The Muppets*, as beloved as they are, use inappropriate violence to a great extent, and don't even attempt to moralize the story.

Sit-coms are often here today and gone tomorrow, so it is rare that the effects of one particular sit-com will be long remembered. However, throughout their televised history, one factor has remained constant—slapstick violence continues to be used as a means of attracting viewers. One of the most recent sit-coms to rely heavily on slapstick violence is *Sledge Hammer!*, a police comedy that averaged 58 acts of violence per hour.[8] Violence in prime time is as old as George Burns and will continue to be used in humorous TV shows and movies because viewers are desensitized to the harmful effects of violence within the context of comedy.

Who is Responsible and Who Will Pay?

The NCTV is asking TV stations that carry war cartoons promoting war toys to provide a balance of information to children about the harmful effects of war toys. To date, TV stations have not voluntarily complied with NCTV's request. More than a few national organizations have a vested interest in seeing that their program-length war cartoons and humorous programs remain on the air. The president of Toy Manufacturers of America said that it would oppose any research or governmental action on the effects of violent toys.

Television and movies are not the only culprits to blame for using too much violence in cartoons and humorous programs. The print media is also violent, whether it is a piece of fiction, such as comic strip, or a news story as documentation of what is happening in the real world. The print media, however, has built-in protections that film media does not. Children who can't read can't experience killing, robberies, kidnappings and rape. But they can experience them just by turning on the TV or watching a film.

The appeal of cartoons and slapstick humor depends on movement and sounds in TV and movies. Cartoons, though often boring to adults, attract young viewers because they are not logical. Cartoons are not hemmed in by adult thinking. For essentially the same reason, slapstick humor appeals not only to children, but also to the "kid" in many adults. It is highly illogical, often contrived and very improbable. Children and adults can dispense with rational thought, lower their guard, and be readily entertained.

Human beings must learn, as children, to handle their aggressive tendencies. During this learning process, it is harmful for children to see violence in others, in life or on the screen. While most adults have better impulse control than they had as children, not all of us have a handle on our aggressive impulses simply because we have achieved "adult" status. The situations adults face can try our best impulse controls. Children desperately need role models with better impulse control than He-Man, Wile E. Coyote, and the Three Stooges to live happy and peaceful adult lives. It is time for this generation of adult Americans to assume responsibility for the next generation, a generation currently raised with many violent media characters as role models.

12
Seeing Is Believing

Children believe to be real any event they see on TV that could happen in real life. As a result, they are more vulnerable to the social message of television. As children get older, they adopt new definitions of television "reality" but still believe that what they see on TV represents something that "probably" happens in the world. The realistic style of many programs contributes to this effect; and **since children tend to identify with characters on TV, they are more apt to treat the televised world as real.**

Thus, children who are constantly exposed to the television message that violence is acceptable, if not the preferred action, cannot help but absorb this into their minds and hearts.

The power of television to communicate feelings can be dangerous. The stimulation of an emotion in this type of situation where it has no real-world consequences can result in a *desensitizing* of feeling. Researchers have found that televised violence makes children more tolerant of aggression in others and less emotionally responsive to violence themselves. **An 11 year-old interviewed by Newsweek stated, "You see so much violence that it's meaningless. If I saw someone really get killed it wouldn't be a big deal. I guess I'm turning into a hard rock."**[1]

It certainly is a shame to hear of a child of that age being so corrupted by the medium that we as parents, perhaps unwittingly, thrust upon them. Violence, even death are so common on television that viewers tend to think of it as routine.

Eighteen members of a New York city youth gang stabbed to death a young boy they believed to be a member of a rival gang, at odds with theirs over rights to a local swimming pool. When asked why he did the stabbing, one participant replied in a matter of fact way, "I always wanted to know what it would be like to stick a knife through bones. After I stabbed that guy, I told him, 'thank you.'"[2]

In another incident two teenage girls strangled a seven-year-old boy. They took him to an attic, used their hands to kill him, covered the body with a blanket and hid it under the floor planks. They had planned the crime months in advance, after seeing something similar done in a gangster movie. Their purpose: to see what death is really like.[3]

Stabbing, strangling, and violent death are not routine occurrences in life. Has television instilled this morbid curiosity in its viewers? Do they think that real life is robbing them of what they believe is an experience they deserve?

"Continuous exposure of children's minds to scenes of crime and brutality has a deeper effect on them than is generally realized . . . people develop a toleration of pain and an accompanying indifference to it," warns Psychiatrist Frederick S. Wertham. **"And most frightening of all, they don't recognize this is happening."[4]**

They don't realize that they are being desensitized because the violence they see on television rarely, if ever, shows its own realities and consequences. Television death produces little or no pain or discomfort and almost never produces any permanent disfigurement or other enduring physical consequences. Televised violence often leads to quick death, and injuries short of death aren't taken seriously. A victim may be beaten, stabbed, or shot and "left to die." The next scene pictures him in a sparkling-white hospital bed in a private room, thankful to be alive, joking through gritted teeth, and apparently feeling few after-effects. The short and long range consequences of serious injury are never shown. Thus, pain, fear, time lost from a job, the high cost of medical care, and the anguish of family members are not part of the television program, nor is crippling, or drawn-out dying.

The viewer has been sidetracked by *antiseptic violence* and impersonality of violence victims.

What Is Desensitization?

Watching violence has a desensitizing and brutalizing effect on people—children and adults alike, proved one psychological experiment. "By 'desensitizing,' I mean that individuals brought up by kindly parents will at first be shocked and horrified when they see one person committing an act of violence against another," says Dr. Benjamin Spock in the November 1987 issue of *Redbook*. "But if they continue to see violence regularly, they will gradually begin to take it for granted as standard human behavior. It has been calculated that the average American young adult has seen more than 50,000 murders or attempted murders on television (including cartoon shows) by the age of 18. That will produce a high degree of desensitization in the long run. This does not mean, however, that a child brought up by parents who are kind and caring will be turned into a thug by watching on-screen violence. But everyone, tough or gentle, will be moved bit by bit in the direction of insensitivity, cynicism and harshness . . . We are surely creating the climate for more such cruelty through the amount of violence that is offered as 'entertainment.' "[5]

157

Repeated exposure to television violence can produce insensitivity to cruelty and violence because it gradually changes the viewers' emotional responses and increases the feeling that violent behavior is normal and appropriate for many circumstances.

There are two branches to the theory of desensitization. The first states that one who is desensitized or insensitive to violence will seek higher and higher levels of violence to obtain his desired level of arousal. In other words, a child who is no longer excited by watching cartoon characters bop each other may progress to human violence viewing to satisfy his subconscious urge for violence. The theory when expanded through the most violent programming available contends that the viewer will then begin to exhibit aggressive personal behavior of increasing harshness—all in an effort to satisfy the "need" begun as watching a few cartoons.

Emotional and physiological responses to other scenes of violence toughen the individual, as do responses to other stimuli. As a result of laboratory studies of changes in skin temperature in response to violence, it was concluded that arousal heightens the likeliness of a person to behave aggressively. Later studies demonstrated that increasing a subject's general arousal increases the probability of aggressive behavior.

Erma Bombeck sums this up in her own special way. She is quoted as having written an angry letter to the television networks that went like this: **"During a single evening I saw twelve people shot, two tortured, one dumped into a swimming pool, two cars explode, a rape, and a man who crawled two blocks with a knife in his stomach.** Do you know something? I didn't feel anger or shock or horror or excitement or repugnance. The truth is I didn't feel. Through repeated assaults of one violent act after another, you have taken from me something I valued—something that contributed to my compassion and caring—the instinct to feel."[6]

There are many kinds of violence, aside from the physical, that play into the pattern of desensitization. Verbal violence (threats and insults), perceptual violence (noise and visual overload) and emotional violence (attacking dignity and worth) fit into this category. Psychologists say that the TV child develops a thick-skinned detachment, a cynical outlook. Constantly exposed to the bloody punch or push, the noise, and the rough language of TV, children learn to accept violence. What is amazing and shameful is the ease with which people accept violence as being not only possible, but probable and "OK."

Ladies' Home Journal Articles Editor Sondra Forsythe Enos summarized that "The American people appear to be unshockable now, desensitized even to genuine brutality—not to mention the lack of simple civility and possessed of an insatiable appetite for whatever might once have been thought unsavory, crude, crass, and even decadent. At a moment in history when we are supposedly becoming more conservative, more mindful of enduring values, our popular culture is becoming flashier, trashier, more vulgar and exploitative."[7]

The Bad Samaritan

The second theory of desensitization deals with acceptance of violence in life as normal, because of the large amounts viewed on television. Although a fair amount of violence viewing might be required to affect an adult's attitude, it has been proven that young children's willingness to accept aggressive behavior of others can be increased by even brief exposures to violent film clips.

In one experiment the comparison was made of the emotional responses of two groups of boys between the ages of 5 and 14 to a graphically violent television program. One group had seen little or no television in the previous two years. The other group had watched an average of 42 hours per week for two years. As the boys viewed an eight minute sequence from the Kirk Douglas movie about boxing, *Champion*, their emotional responses were recorded on a physiograph. This instrument measures heart action, respiration, perspiration and other body responses. According to their measured reactions, the boys with a history of heavy television viewing were significantly less aroused by what they saw. The researchers concluded that their desensitization was a result of the many violent programs that they had seen in their 42 hours per week.[8]

A disturbing possibility exists that the television experience has not merely blurred the distinctions between the real and the unreal for steady viewers, but that by doing so, it has dulled their sensitivities to actual events. Once television fantasy becomes incorporated into the viewers' reality, the real world takes on a tinge of fantasy or dullness because it fails to confirm the expectations created by televised "life." Children and adults who are heavy television viewers are exposed to so much violence that they become habituated or desensitized to violence in general. "Normal" people begin to accept violence as an ordinary companion in their lives. A kind of psychological "tuning out" takes place as compared to one's normal response to this type of event.

Have you read newspaper articles telling about fewer and fewer citizens who are willing to help someone being attacked or assaulted? In some cases the victim is within their range of help. One illustration of this lack of concern for others is the Kitty Genovese case. Kitty was a young woman living in a Brooklyn apartment complex who was assaulted, raped, and murdered. The crimes were committed on Kitty while she was in the complex and lasted longer than a half an hour. Apparently normal people did nothing while just below their windows a man sexually disfigured and killed the young woman. Subsequent investigation revealed that 40 people heard her screams, but no one did anything to help her. No one telephoned the police (even anonymously), or called out in an attempt to scare the killer away.

"When one of the witnesses went to the window of her apartment, she could not get a clear view of the murder taking place on the sidewalk below. 'Turn off the lights, dumbell,' her husband is reported to have suggested, 'then you can see.' She did, and they both pulled up chairs to the window to watch the show."[9]

Another example of Bad Samaritanism can be seen in the account of an incident in a Massachusetts tavern when a woman was raped by a gang of men on a pooltable while onlookers cheered.[10]

And recently, a Pennsylvania woman was criminally assaulted and raped near a high school on a Sunday afternoon. Several people were reported to be visible to the young woman, but no one came to her aid.[11]

Is it the fact that they have seen violence hundreds of times on television that makes these Bad Samaritans neglect to rush to the aid of a victim? Are they, perhaps, having trouble distinguishing reality from media fantasy?

Journalist Jane Margold was driving home one night when a man crawled into the street in front of her. She screeched to a stop and then, stunned, just sat there for a moment. When she cautiously went to the man, she found that he had been stabbed several times and was in danger of dying. His assailant was nowhere to be seen. In describing the event, Jane said that she flipped into a media version of herself. She had never faced anything like it before and had no direct feelings. Instead, playing through her mind were images of similar events she had seen on television or in films. The media images superceded her own responses, even to the point of removing her from the event. She didn't experience herself as being there. She was seeing the event, but between her and it, floating in her mind, was an image of an implanted reality. She thought such thoughts as: "This is real; there's a wounded man lying here in front of me, bleeding to death, yet I have no feeling. It seems like a movie." Without feeling, she performed mechanical acts— comforted the man, directed traffic, summoned police and an ambulance. She became extremely efficient, but throughout, she had the sense of performing a script.[12]

After seeing violence dealt out day after day on fictional programs presented in a realistic style within a realistic framework, viewers incorporate it into their reality, in spite of the fact that while they are watching television, they know that the programs are fictional. **Violence in the real world seems more acceptable after you've seen much greater violence on television or in the movies.**

As Christians, we must assess the degree to which we have been desensitized. Remember, this happens without our even knowing it. Sin is more than simply committing immoral acts. It includes everything to which we consciously choose to expose ourselves.

Antiseptic Violence

In an effort to stop public criticism and government control, the networks have attempted to *sanitize* their violent programming. Television characters usually die quickly and quietly or out of camera range. A study commissioned by the U.S. Conference of Mayors showed that police programs portraying violence in an antiseptic manner, with little "blood or guts," misleads the public about the pain and suffering caused by the violence. Viewers must be made aware that pain and suffering result from a bullet or stab wound, and that weapons are truly instruments of deadly force.

"When death does result from a violent televised act, it is short and sweet. Blood does not flow, organs are not smashed, the bowels do not move in one last desperate reflex," states Frank Mankiewicz and Joel Serdlow, "The exit wounds of bullets which in reality are often the size of a dinner plate, are not visible. Instead, viewers see only surgically clean and usually bloodless entry wounds which miracuously never hit arteries. The true physical dynamics of death are ignored in favor of clean, sterile, motionless bodies."[13]

Blow To The Head

The most frequent example of violence in prime-time television is the "blow to the head with a blunt instrument." There is hardly a prime-time hour free of an example or two of this favorite method of violence. Someone gets hit over the head with a chair or the butt of a gun, an

assailant will be felled with a karate chop to the neck, or a hero will be "conked on the bean." In each instance, the result is the same: The person hit on the head is rendered unconscious for a short while, then awakens. The time for total recovery is brief.

The message which the television delivers is clear: a blow with all of one's might to the head of another with a blunt object is a very efficient way to stop someone without serious injury. This is not so. Physicians report that blows to the head regularly cause serious injury. In addition to death and paralysis some effects include temporary or permanent loss of motor abilities, the inability to speak or understand speech or symbols, convulsions, dizziness, or chronic headaches as well as emotional problems such as anxiety, fear, irritability, depression, and paranoia.

Even when death occurs, television sanitizes it. No funeral directors are pictured. Few mourners are shown, if any, and the extent of their loss is often pictured in a dramatic shot of a single tear.

As a matter of fact, television inadvertently teaches us that people seldom die. Even the youngest children know the hero will walk away from the violent crash because he is the "star" and there is another show to do for next week. Soap operas are famous (or infamous) for reviving dead characters, days or even years after their demise.

On television, violence is virtually the sole cause of death, but performs its service quickly and the victim is whisked off camera. Whether he goes to the hospital or the morgue is of little concern in most programming as long as it is done in an antiseptic manner so as not to offend the more delicate of those who crave their daily fix of violence.

Rape

In the spectrum of television violence, rape deserves particular mention. Journalism professor Caryl Rivers watched two hours of televised rape scenes for the *New York Times* and came away shocked: "the rape of *Hawaii Five-0* was not horrifying, not ugly. 'Titillating' is the word for the way it was presented. Lovingly the camera stalked the rapists' victims, it peeped at shapely legs in miniskirts, leered at a wiggly walk, watched a swaying bottom. It made rape seem like a subject for a *Playboy* centerfold, an incident without terror and pain . . . This sanitized portrayal contrasts completely with the brutality and lingering scars that accompany real rape."[14]

Industry spokesmen argue with some justification that they cannot show violence in all of its horrible details and consequences. This was proven when the *Medical Story* series too realistically portrayed an operation, and viewers tuned out in sufficient numbers for the show to be canceled. Obviously, people do not wish to see the details of life's unpleasantness and cruelties on the living room set. But sanitizing the violence as television presently does gives viewers a false perspective which, even if it is subconscious, serves to desensitize them.

Who Are The Victims?

As violence ignores causes, it ignores effects. When a castle is besieged, we may or may not be shown a man screaming as he is hurled from the battlements. We almost never recognize and identify with minor characters before they disppear in agony. The victim is not depicted as a man but as an object, or, if an enemy, as one of "them" and therefore expendable. But he is not an object. He had a mother and father who loved him, and brothers, sisters and other relatives to whom he was dear. He might have had a wife and children. He might have loved cats, fishing, and roasted chestnuts, and detested bedbugs, skittles, and turnips. In short, he was a human being, and if he is to be killed for our amusement, we should appreciate him as such. Many times a burglary is shown in which the gas station owner or the proprietor of the candy store is killed. Once he is dead, the audience forgets him and follows the "important" character, the teen-ager who has shot him. The sympathies of the audience are directed to the murderer's problems. The shopkeeper has ceased to exist, as if he was never more than an excuse for the "protagonist's" troubles to center on briefly. This fictional shopkeeper, who may be on the screen only for the few moments it takes to rob and kill him, is every bit as real as his fictional murder. As a result of his death, his wife may have a heart attack, the business may fail, his mother may be forced to go on welfare and his children into foster homes. Unrealistic? Not at all. This kind of chain of events is not uncommon when senseless, violent disaster strikes. To a child, a mugging or killing is presented as exhilarating action. Children should know that these victims are people and they and their families may suffer lifelong pain, grief, and ruinous expense, not in any way commensurate with the monetary thrill the culprit enjoys. Violence acts as an "equalizer" and unless children can rid themselves of the impersonality, the lack of interest that converts victims to things or "them," we are bringing up a society with deadened perceptions and diminished humanity.

This lack of sensitivity about pain and death cannot help but contribute to the increase of real violence in our culture.

13

New Breed Of Criminal And His Copycat Crime

"We have silently passed an amendment to the sixth commandment: 'thou shalt not kill,but it is perfectly all right for you to enjoy watching other people do it,'" writes author Dave Schwantes.[1]

High action content is arousing to television viewers. Arousal dissipates quickly, but for a period of time as long as a few days after exposure, a child may act more aggressively because he has been aroused by TV violence. In rare instances, such arousal may collide with circumstances to produce tragic results. It is these results that we are addressing in this chapter.

Television violence may be imitated, either impulsively or when environmental circumstances invite or condone acts that have been modeled on TV. Many children and adolescents thus gain the potential for acting in more aggressive and antisocial ways as a result of their exposure. TV violence conveys attitudes and values about violent aggression and antisocial behavior. Although older children and adolescents discount particular content as being "just a story," they describe roles, role relationships, and interactions of characters as highly realistic. Admired characters are presumed to behave in appropriate or desirable ways, and their approval of aggression or antisocial behavior elevates it in the eyes of young viewers.

What Is Television Teaching?

No other experience in a child's life permits quite so much intake while demanding so little outflow as does watching television. The father of a five-year-old relates, *"My son and I were lying on the bed together the other night watching a program about labor unrest in Cornwall, and he was absolutely fascinated. I said to him, 'Would you like me to explain this to you?' and he said, 'No, Daddy, I'm just watching.' "*

The mother of another five-year-old observed that her son went into an apparent trance when he watched TV. "He just gets locked into what is happening on the screen," she said. "He's totally, absolutely absorbed when he watches TV. He doesn't hear me. To get his attention I have to turn off the set." TV heroes such as Hunter, Magnum, O'Hara, Spenser, and the officers of *Houston Knights* and *Miami Vice* have replaced parents, teachers, and clergy as models for proper conduct and behavior in society.

Dr. Benjamin Spock said that he became convinced of the dangers of television violence after an experienced nursery school teacher told him how she saw children bopping each other over the head. When she intervened, a child responded indignantly, "That's what the Three Stooges do." Spock said that children, especially young ones, would pattern themselves after violent behavior as easily as they imitate good behavior. They believe whatever adults do is OK.

Do we really want our children using McCall of *The Equalizer* or Spenser as role models for future behavior? NCTV named Walt Disney's *Sidekick* as the worst new violent program on television in 1986.[2] This program averaged 43 acts of violence per episode. It featured a policeman's 12 year-old adopted son who used karate kicks and martial arts violence against numerous villains to help his dad solve each week's crime caper. Is this the type of game that we want to see our children playing on the school playground?

Who Are The Heroes?

Former pro-football star, and current television star, Alex Karras wrote an article for *TV Guide* about who the real men are on TV. He pointed out that roles like Mike Hammer and B.A. Baracus (Mr. T) portray negative macho roles. Karras says he is concerned about TV heroes who love violent battles and beating someone up, "characteristic of animals, not real men." *Hunter, Miami Vice, Fall Guy,* and *Dallas'* J. R. are all faulted by Karras for their superficial and shallow violence.[3]

In a January 1987 news release, NCTV cited *Mike Hammer* for airing the worst single TV episode of the season. In the first hour of the suspect episode, a woman strips down totally naked in front of Mike Hammer and asks him to go to bed with her. At the end of the program she slips a gun up to his head, while kissing him, in order to kill him. Instead, he kills her by shooting her in the abdomen with a gun he has hidden in his coat pocket. This provides quite an example for an impressionable teenage boy. (This episode was re-run in January of 1988.)

CBS's *Tour of Duty,* a series about the war in Vietnam, contained the highest level of physical violence of the Fall 1987 programming. NCTV chose to praise this series for portraying Vietnamese rebels in human terms and usually focusing on the tragedy of war rather than on violence itself.[4] This opinion aside, the program displays vivid scenes of the "blood and guts" variety, killings of every style, and a wide array of weaponry for our youngsters to imitate on the school yard battleground.

Says professor Robert E. Gould, M.D., **"This distorted portrayal of violence, making violence appear as a very effective way to deal with conflict, is having a harmful effect on our society** . . . **Using violence as a means of fantasy entertainment is a bad idea even for normal adults and still worse for children and adolescents."**[5]

Playing with violent toys "increases the risks that children are going to use aggression in real-life . . . the violent toys serve as a way of rehearsing the violent behavior seen on television," declares Syracuse University's Dr. Arnold Goldstein. However, statistics show that there has been a 600 percent increase in war toy sales over the last three years.

A substantial amount of research suggests we are influenced by visual media more than we realize or are prepared to admit. The individual effects of TV and film violence depend largely on each person's psychological and moral make-up. In a recent *Christianity Today* article, Randy Frame points out, "We can be thankful that not everyone who sees *Taxi Driver* will be affected in the same way as John Hinckley."[6]

The Link

The number of juveniles arrested for serious and violent crimes increased 1600 percent between the years 1952 and 1972 according to FBI figures. A study made at the Center for Studies in Criminology and Criminal Law at the University of Pennsylvania, two large groups of urban youth were compared, one of which reached adulthood in the 1960's and the other in the 1970's. The more recent group showed three times the rate of murder and other violence than the 1960's group. Since the period between 1952 and 1972 was the time when television became ascendent in the lives of American children (children who reached adulthood in 1960 are still generally considered the pre-television generation), and since the programs children watch are saturated with crime and destruction, it seems reasonable to search for a link between the two. The truly repugnant, sadistic, amazingly various violence appearing on television programming must surely have effects upon children's behavior, however subtle. It is particularly difficult for some parents to accept the idea that television instigates aggressive behavior when its function in the home is so different. Here television keeps children quiet and passive, cuts down on loud, boisterous play, prevents outbursts between brothers and sisters, and in general keeps children occupied.

But, if it is not the violent content of television programs that leads to violent behavior, is it merely a coincidence that the entry of television into the American home brought in its wake one of the worst epidemics of juvenile violence in the nation's history? There are indeed reasons to believe that television is deeply implicated in the new upsurge of juvenile aggression, particularly in the development of a new and frightening breed of juvenile offenders.

Kids And Guns

The number of kids using and being harmed by guns is rising at an alarming rate. The most recent figures released by the U.S. Dept. of Justice showed that more than 27,000 youths between 12 and 15 were handgun victims in 1985, up from an average of 16,500 for each of the previous three years reports *Newsweek*. **City streets have become flooded with unregistered and untraceable handguns, available to anyone of any age with a bit of cash.** In New York, revolvers can be bought on street corners for $25 or "rented" for an evening until the teen can raise the cash through a mugging or robbery. Approximately 80,000 youth in 600 gangs in Los

Angeles protect their turf with black-market Uzi submachine guns and Russian-made AK-47 assault rifles. Last year, over 380 people were slain by this city's "baby gangsters" who battle each other over drug profits, or kill on a dare or over taunts that become battle cries. Children who live outside of urban areas have an even cheaper source of firearms—dad's closet. Guns seem to be enjoying a new chic and a study in California showed that 38 percent of all households contain a gun.

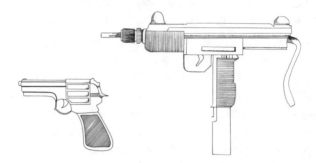

Americans Like Violence

Of all the people in industrialized nations, Americans are the most prone to violence. Between 1963 and 1973 when the war in Vietnam took 46,212 lives, firearms in the U.S. killed 86,644 civilians. In 1980 there were 8 reported handgun murders in England and 1,012 in the U.S. The Bureau of the Census reported that between 1974 and 1983 the number of aggravated assaults increased by 6 percent, forcible rape by 26 percent, robbery by 2 percent, and child abuse by 48 percent. William F. Fore, *The Christian Century* editor at large, states that ". . . for years the evidence has been slowly accumulating. Now the verdict is as clear as the evidence that links smoking to cancer: Violence in the media is causing violence in society."[7]

Nowhere is the proliferation of firearms among youths more startling than in city high schools. *Newsweek* reports the results of a survey of weapon use ordered by Circuit Judge Ellen Heller in Baltimore. Of 390 high schoolers polled: 64 percent knew someone who had carried a handgun within the preceding six months; 60 percent knew someone who had been shot, threatened, or robbed at gunpoint in their school; almost 50 percent of males admitted to having carried a handgun at least once.[8]

Today, packing a pistol is a symbol of status and power that others quickly imitate. Students with no criminal intent start carrying guns to protect themselves from gun toting class bullies. Hallway disputes that were once settled with fists now end in a burst of fire and a bloody corpse. Outbursts like these are attributed to a society too tolerant of TV violence. **We show that fighting is glamorous on TV—it is rewarded and chosen by the hero as the first solution to a problem.** It is our responsibility to point out the fallacy of this picture to our children and society in general.

New Breed of Criminal

A frightening new breed of juvenile offender appeared in American society for the first time in the 1970's. The *New York Times* classifies him as "the child-murderer who feels no remorse and is scarcely conscious of his acts." Two professors in the *International Journal of Law and Psychiatry* have assigned a name to this new category of juveniles: "non-empathic murderers," defining them as "children who lack the psychological ability to put themselves in the place of another." One such killer, charged within a year with the deaths of an elderly woman and a six-year-old girl, was quoted: "I don't know the girl so why should I have any feelings about what happened to her?"[9]

Law officers and authorities blame lenient laws for the incidence of these crimes. The harshest action facing a youth under 16 who commits murder in many states is confinement for up to 18 months in a public or private institution. The juvenile offenders of today harbor the arrogant belief that the law will be lenient toward them, that they can literally get away with murder. The common factor characterizing these juveniles who kill, torture and rape seems to be a form of emotional detachment that allows them to commit unspeakable crimes with a complete absence of guilt or remorse. It is as if they were dealing with inanimate objects rather than human beings. A psychiatrist connected with the Brooklyn Family Court describes these children as showing "a total lack of guilt and lack of respect for life. To them another person is a thing—they are wild organisms who cannot allow anyone to stand in their way." Is it possible that all of the hours these disturbed children spend watching television—being involved in an experience that dulls the boundaries between the real and the unreal, that projects human images and the illusion of human feelings, while requiring no human responses from the viewer—encourages them to detach themselves from their antisocial acts in a new and horrible way?

Dr. Thomas Radecki referred to over 700 studies and reports on the issue of television violence when he cited television as the number one cause of real-life violence. He estimates that "25-50 percent of the violence in our society is coming from the culture of violence being taught by our entertainment media"[10] He pointed to research showing that adults are as strongly affected as children.

Copy-cat Crime, A Journal Of Violence

Aside from "street" crime, this new breed of criminal, adolescent and adult alike has been indulging in an increasing number of "copy-cat" crimes. The name comes from the perpetrator's imitation either direct or implied of a model crime. For our purpose, we are dealing with crimes instigated by television programming.

The observation that television distorts reality far more for a disturbed child than for a normal child may bear a relation to the epidemic of juvenile crime in recent decades. For there is no doubt that the children involved in serious crimes today are not normal. In many instances their histories reveàl a background of poverty, degradation, neglect, scholastic failure, frustration, family pathology . . . and heavy television viewing. But while poverty and family pathology did not appear for the first time in American society in the 1970's, a frightening new breed of juvenile offender did. With frequency, newspapers report juvenile crimes that fill the hearts of normal readers with horror and disbelief: ten and twelve-year-old muggers preying on the elderly, casually torturing and murdering their helpless victims. "The total banishment of violence from the television screen will not mitigate the dehumanizing effects of long periods of television viewing upon

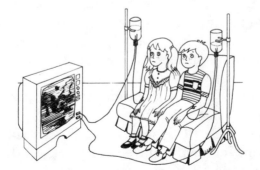

emotionally disturbed children," asserted Marie Winn, "For the problem is not that they learn how to commit violence from watching violence on television (although perhaps they sometimes do), but that television conditions

175

them to deal with real people as if they were on a television screen. Thus they are able to turn them off quite simply, with a knife, or a gun or a chain, with as little remorse as if they were turning off a television set."[11]

The Doomsday Flight

Perhaps the first widely imitated television crime was portrayed in *The Doomsday Flight*, a filmed drama broadcast by NBC. In the film, a bomb is placed aboard a transcontinental plane by a deranged man who keeps teasing officials with information about his deadly act. The program ends happily when the pilot lands the plane at an altitude above that at which the bomb is triggered to explode. The first bomb threat came while the film was still on the air. Within the next 24 hours, there were four more threats, and by the end of the week at least 8 hoax calls had been received. The film's author, Rod Serling said that he held himself responsible and regretted writing the script. Then, in 1975 another round of threats struck panic into French aviation when *The Doomsday Flight* appeared on that country's television screens.

In Hartford City, Indiana, four men chose a home at random and blasted four brothers to death with shotguns. They later testified that viewing the TV version of the Charles Manson murders, *Helter Skelter*, had influenced them to commit the crime.

22 youthful offenders reported actually trying criminal techniques they had seen on television revealed the Heller and Polsky studies. 19 of them said their television inspired crimes were carried out successfully and without detection. Another 22 men reported contemplating crimes they had seen on television and more than half of the total sample, 52 percent, felt that television had changed their thoughts or beliefs.In a small study of 35 offenders which the authors considered a pilot for the project, more

than a third of these boys indicated that they were consciously aware of acting out the techniques of a crime which they had previously seen "demonstrated" on television![12]

One of the most ghastly imitative crimes occurred in Boston after ABC broadcast the movie *Fuzz*. In the movie, a group of teenagers killed a derelict by dousing him with gasoline and setting him on fire. Two nights later, 24 year old Evelyn Wagler's car ran out of gas in the Roxbury section of Boston. As she was returning from the service station with a full can of gasoline, she was attacked by a gang of youths who poured the gasoline over her and set her aflame. Her murderers were never apprehended.

Nine-Year-Old Girl Is Attacked

In 1974 nine-year-old Olivia Neimi was attacked by three older girls and a boy on a beach in San Francisco in the process of which she was artifically raped with a bottle. Four days before the incident the movie *Born Innocent*, portraying a girl being similarly raped with a plumbers helper, was aired by an NBC San Francisco TV station. Olivia's mother and her lawyer, Marvin Lewis, claimed that Olivia's assault was provoked by the movie and demanded $11 million damages from NBC and the affiliate station due to the broadcaster's alleged negligence in showing the movie, especially during prime-time when children and adolescents comprise a fair share of the audience. The legal term for the alleged negligence is "vicarious liability," based on the presumed incitement of a criminal act if it is vividly depicted in a book, TV show, or other medium, the source of that depiction being responsible for damages to the victim. The First Amendment was the major argument of the defense lawyers of NBC. They argued that a ruling in favor of Niemi would stifle journalists, broadcasters, and publishers. Marvin Lewis argued that our Forefathers did not design the First Amendment to protect a graphic portrayal of the gang rape of a child before a nationwide children's audience. Many suits and countersuits followed as well as a series of actions which involved two rulings by California's highest court and one by the US Supreme court. The negligence suit was ultimately thrown out of court in August of 1978, before witnesses were even heard because Judge Robert Dossee ruled that the plaintiff had to prove that the network intended its viewers to imitate the violent sexual attack depicted. With the case being treated by the judge as a strict First Amendment Case, Marvin Lewis could not win. It was not feasible to prove that NBC intended its viewers to copy the rape scene. Note: One week later, the US Supreme Court ruled that Niemi was entitled to a court hearing.[13]

Some other examples of crimes copied from TV include a nine-year-old's effort to slip his teacher a box of poisoned chocolates and a seven-year-old's use of ground glass in the family stew.

The fatal crossbow shooting of woman took place two days after an episode of *Hart to Hart* on television featured an assassination with such a weapon. Michelle Rae Powers, 30, was getting into her car outside her Tulsa apartment when she was mortally wounded in the chest by a 16 inch projectile fired from a crossbow. In their book *Remote Control*, Frank Mankiewicz and Joel Swerdlow state, "Defenders of the television industry insist that such crimes are committed by mentally unstable people who would have done something violent, illegal, or crazy whether or not television existed, and quote Herminio Traviesas, NBC's director of continuity (the chief censor who decides what does and does not get on the air) as saying, "You can't judge things by the few nuts."

The authors then proceed to list a series of incidents that researchers discovered:

In San Diego, a 19 year-old boy chopped his parents and his sister to death and crippled his brother with an axe. Prosecutors and police officials familiar with the case say he acted after seeing a made-for-television movie about Lizzie Borden, notorious for the axe murder of her parents. The honor student and athlete discussed the movie with his classmates in the days after it was shown.

Three weeks after the broadcast of a made-for-television murder movie in 1973, a 17 year-old boy, who said he had "memorized the film to the last detail," admitted to re-enacting the crime when he murdered a young woman. Police said she had been raped, her head had been bludgeoned, and her throat was cut—just as in the film.

In New York City a taxi driver held up a bar and killed three people. Caught by police, he said his crime had been modeled after a recent television show.

In Baltimore, an ex-GI in fatigues shot and killed five co-workers with an M-1 rifle; police later discovered that he had purchased some chocolate bars at the same time he bought the rifle. He made the purchases one week after a prime-time television program had portrayed a fatigue-clad veteran who munched chocolate bars while shooting at passers-by.

A popular crime show depicted an urban killer who slashed the throats of Skid Row "winos." A few days later, in Los Angeles, a wino was discovered with his throat slit. It was the forerunner of the "Skid Row Slasher's" reign of terror which claimed numerous victims, all killed in the same way.

In Montreal, thieves used a 10mm anti-aircraft gun to rob a Brinks truck of $1.6 million. Their modus operandi closely paralleled events on a recent prime-time crime program.

A 71 year-old Seattle man tried to rob a bank and walked right into the hands of the police. "It looked easy on television," he said.

In Lexington, S.C., a young couple picked up a hitchhiker, shot him, and staged a car crash in which his body was burned. The woman then tried to claim insurance on the victim's life. The Lexington County Sheriff believes the crime had "something to do" with an episode of a private-eye program, *Barnaby Jones*, with an identical murder-for-insurance plot shown just before the killing.

A Dallas police sergeant recites numerous examples of crimes he believes to be directly inspired by television, and focuses particularly on a gang of juveniles who succeeded in cracking the steering-column lock on new cars. When asked how they had acquired the technique, the boys told him they had seen it on episodes of a police program.[14]

The Burning Bed

In 1984, at least three people suffered following the NBC movie *The Burning Bed*. Joseph Brandt, 39, waited in his estranged wife's Milwaukee driveway one night with a gas can and a lighter. When Sharon arrived, her husband stepped forward with gas and flame. Screams brought their two sons running to the backyard where Sharon lay critically burned. Vietnam vet Brandt, dressed in fatiques and a mud-smeared face yelled, "Look at your mother now!" It was apparently a gruesome case of life imitating art imitating life. Shortly before he assaulted his wife, Brandt said he had watched *The Burning Bed*, the true story of a battered wife who ended 13 years of marital torment by torching the gasoline-soaked bed containing her sleeping husband. Brandt told police that the show inspired him to "scare his wife."

In Quincy, Mass., a husband angered by the same movie beat his wife senseless, "He told her he wanted to get her before she got him." And, in Chicago, a battered wife watched the show—then shot her husband.[15]

More Examples

More recent examples of this type of crime can be found in magazines and newspapers daily.

In August 1987 a 12-year-old boy in Corpus Christi, Texas, wounded a stock-broker on a crowed downtown street. What most shocked the victim was the way the kid blew the smoke out of his barrel, Clint Eastwood style, then got on his bike and rode away. A 10 year-old Arkansas boy was admitted to the intensive care unit after being shot in the neck by a friend who was mimicking a television commercial for the Laser Tag game. The Laser Tag game is one in which each player has a gun that shoots a beam of light. Each player wears a censor that beeps and lights when hit. The boys were good friends who told police that they saw people on TV shooting at each other so decided to do the same thing. The 11 year-old who did the shooting thought the .22 caliber rifle that he used was unloaded.

One problem is that often network officials refuse to heed the advice of the public or concerned groups and run suspect programming. In the case of *The Doomsday Flight*, the Air Line Pilots Association urged NBC to cancel, warning that the drama might cause an act of sabotage. As we said before, the first bomb threat came while the program was still on the air. Much controversy surrounded the airing of *Born Innocent*. And, it was reported that the Minneapolis CBS station received 7,000 calls and the Portland, Oregon CBS station had 4,000 asking them not to show *Exorcist II*. In spite of the public concern, the movie was broadcast and a four-year-old girl was killed by her mother after the two watched the program.

Alberta Siegal, a member of the Surgeon General's committee stated, "Television time is sold to sponsors on the conviction that although an Ajax ad will not guarantee that the viewer will buy the product, it raises the probability that he will. Social scientists would simply make the same claim for filmed or televised violence, whether fictitious or real. Viewing the carnage does not guarantee that the viewer will go forth and do likewise but it raises the probability that he will."[16]

Thomas Radecki noted in a government hearing—**"My conservative estimate, based on extrapolations from the research, would suggest that over a thousand murders every year are the direct result of TV violence. This number could easily be as high as 5,000 or more every year of the 20,000 murders nation-wide being directly or indirectly due to TV violence."**[17]

14

Killer Drillers And Plasmic Perverts

"See bloodthirsty butchers, killer drillers, crazed cannibals, zonked zombies, mutilating maniacs, hemoglobin horrors, plasmic perverts and sadistic slayers slash, strangle, mangle and mutilate bare-breasted beauties in bondage,"[1] announced the advertisement for a film about "gore."

As we have said before, in recent years there has been concern about the problem of media violence, especially after television's home screen began to show scenes of murder and mayhem. Parents, teachers and concerned individuals are now noting a new trend—sexual violence. The use of physical force and violent imagery in a sexual context is disturbing to many, but has become increasing popular as a theme in music and music video, horror movies (especially "slasher" films), and in advertising and commercials.

As few as a half-dozen years ago, Christian parents didn't have to worry about this topic. Films whose content was of this nature were considered pornographic or rated XXX, and access was limited. The expansion of pay cable channels and affordability of videocassette recorders has brought into the average American home what used to be available only at the sleasiest theaters or drive-ins.

Women as Victims

"It's a crime to kill a man; it's sexy to kill a woman,"
notes Linda Bloodworth-Thomason, co-executive producer of Robert Wagner's series for ABC, *Lime Street*.[2]
From the preview of the fresh batch of macho
adventure/dramas this season, it looks like women are
again going to be treated like dirt. The only chance for
a television role for most starlets will be, quite literally,
a one-shot appearance, since the majority of the roles
for women are as victims of sadistic killers. In *Mike
Hammer* sex appears to be free, but women still pay—
usually with their lives. The majority of the victims are
clones of the Hammerettes—sexy-looking young women
in sexy and/or morally dubious lines of work. Women
of "easy virtue" are easily disposable. And nobody seems
to care. "They have to be people who don't matter," one
television scriptwriter said. "That kind of a plot is easy.
You don't have to explain why such a person could die."[3]
The majority of the action series seem to be tapping
into male-fantasy, with beautiful voluptuous women as
victims, usually of a serial killer. Besides hookers, victims
include models, co-eds, teenage runaways, aerobics
instructors and beauty contestants as well as
contemporary working women including all-female rock
groups, saleswomen, and an occasional reporter. It is the
hero's assignment to kill the killer before he kills again.
To solve many of these cases, a female cop has to go
undercover, placing herself in great danger and the hero
in a position to save her in the nick of time. In *MacGruder
& Loud* on ABC, Jenny has posed as a prostitute on
several occasions. The token woman on ABC's *The Fall
Guy* found herself in jail where the women were being
prostituted. NBC's *Miami Vice* has frequent brushes with
threatened beauties, in one instance going undercover as
beauty contest judges to prevent murder.

We authors find it difficult to believe that the average American woman can identify with most of the females they see on prime-time television. Prostitutes? Sexually insatiable young teens? Centerfolds and nude models? Weak women who are easy marks for sadistic criminals? The networks claim that women make up the majority of their viewers, yet they insult the female's intelligence by presenting such programming. It is time to expose the Hollywood producers who are projecting their own idea of bedroom porn into our living rooms. They are perpetuating the myth that women are weak and worthless. We must not permit this to continue. These are not the attitudes that we want to encourage in our young men and certainly not the role models that we prefer for our teenage daughters.

Ethnic Discrimination

The heroine leaped to her death from a cliff rather than be touched by a "lewd black man" in *Birth Of A Nation*. Another dimension to the issue of sexual violence in the media is that of ethnic discrimination. A century-long diet of selected ethnic groups committed sexual violence helped shape public beliefs and attitudes about those groups. The "greaser" westerns of the early 1900's showed Mexicans regularly menacing, kidnapping, and sexually threatening Anglo heroines.

During the 1930's Asian men sexually menacing white women themes prevailed while World War II movies featured the sexual fear of American nurses being captured by Japanese soldiers *(So Proudly We Hail)*. For decades Indians abducted white women, and black pimps beat up their prostitutes. Today the cheap thrills of interracial sexual violence are even more graphic. A black gang terrorizes Nancy Allen in a New York subway in *Dressed to Kill* and Kim Basinger, tied to a pillar and surrounded by lusting Arabs, is saved from this fate worse than death by James Bond in *Never Say Never Again*. Movie makers know what grabs audiences and will disregard any conscience in search of the almighty dollar.

Sex and Violence

In a terror film sex is never shown as making love in the context of a Godly relationship. It is not the pleasurable expression of two people who genuinely love and care for each other in a union blessed by God. *To increase the entertainment value, sex acts are often illicit, premarital or extramarital and end in mutilation.*

Blending sex with violence is a deliberate attempt on the part of the movie makers to manipulate the viewer into feeling the most primitive passions. Scenes used to arouse the sexual drives of the viewers are craftily cut into horror movies, just before graphically violent acts. For example, a young woman seductively removes her clothes to bathe when the night stalker enters and bludgeons her to death. Consider what movie makers are trying to accomplish with such a scene. By showing an attractive girl disrobing, they are trying to arouse the audience to feel lust. Before those lustful feelings subside, the violent act is completed (in this case, the clubbing), so that the audience is manipulated to feel a confusing mixture of desire and fear or repulsion. Blending sex with violence can result in awakening a dangerous new appetite in viewers—a desire to see sexual acts culminate in violence: stranglings, murderous rape or worse.

What is equally disturbing about the abundant use of sexually violent scenes is that in real life, women are almost exclusively the target for sex offenses. Nowhere is it more apparent that women are victims of sex crimes than in the movies. Nearly every woman in a vulnerable position is made a target of some horrific crime. A nurse working the graveyard shift in the local hospital is drowned in a whirlpool bath by the homicidal maniac in *Halloween II*. Though drowning is not a sex crime, it has sexual overtones when by the end of the drowning, the nurse's clothes have been removed. Some scenes from movies that are dangerous combinations of sex with graphic violence or that make victims of women are:

Nightmare
   A woman gets her head chopped off while having sex.
   Using a pick axe, a woman is stabbed repeatedly in the back, while a child watches.

Slayer
   A woman is killed with a pitch fork.
   A woman wakes up with only the head of her husband beside her.

City of the Walking Dead
   The head is graphically blown off a woman.
   A woman's breast is cut off.

Color Me Blood Red
   So that an artist can paint with her blood, a woman is stabbed in the head through her ear.

Blood Tide
   A half-naked woman is being eaten by a skeletal creature.

Blood Feast
   While taking a bath, a woman is stabbed in the eye, then chopped up by the killer.
   A woman's tongue is pulled out of her mouth while she is alive in a graphic rape scene.

All the violent sex scenes in today's horror movies are too numerous to mention. Some of the scenes are too disgusting to describe. The content of today's blood and guts horror movies suggests that movie makers are cashing in on the entertainment value of sex crimes and the victimization of women.

Rape Sometimes OK?

Rape occurred in 18 percent or one in six of the 1987 films.[4] To us this is a very disturbing figure. Since the viewing of violence causes insensitivity, the frequent viewing of women being beaten and raped by men has serious consequences.

If anyone has read this far into our book and still questions the concept of desensitization, the results of a 1987 survey of 1,700 seventh to ninth-graders in Rhode Island should be very interesting. We find them shocking and repulsive! Jacqueline Jackson Kikuchi presented the following findings to the National Symposium on Child Victimization on April 29, 1988:

1. 24 percent of the boys and 16 percent of the girls said it was acceptable for a man to force a woman to have sex with him if he has spent money on her.

2. 65 percent of the boys and 47 percent of the girls said it is acceptable for a man to force a woman to have sex if they have been dating for more than six months.

3. 87 percent of the boys and 79 percent of the girls said rape is OK if a couple is married.

4. 31 percent of the boys and 32 percent of the girls said it would not be improper for a man to rape a woman who has had previous sexual experiences.

5. 50 percent of the students said a woman who walks alone at night and dresses seductively is asking to be raped.

Can you believe that these are the attitudes the media is developing in the 12 year-old boy who will be dating your teenage daughter in a few years? "The types of attitudes evidenced in the survey probably lead to date rape and other forms of sexual assault," said Ms. Kikuchi.[5]

Visual media presentation of women as easy targets for aggressive behavior as a common occurrence should not be allowed. Not only do adolescent boys get a perverted view of human sexuality, but the attitudes have a tendency to make willing victims of teenage girls who are led to believe that they are at fault for what is done to them. We firmly believe that rape, as well as other violent acts, should never be recreated for entertainment purposes.

What Sexual Violence Does To Us.

Media portrayals can promote the view that women desire violence. They can transform sensitive individuals' view of rape to make it seem more acceptable and not such an abhorrent act. Exposure to this kind of material can contribute to changes in their belief structure—and these can be changes for the worst.

Dr. Neil Malamuth, associate professor and chairman of the Department of Communication Studies, University of California has been studying the impact of sexually explicit and sexually violent films and tapes on university students. In some cases portrayals involved what Malamuth calls "the rape myth"—the idea that women enjoy sexual violence, and that it leads to positive consequences. The popular film *Swept Away*, is a good example of this concept. It depicts a woman who falls in love with the man who raped her.

There were differences between the effects on men and women of this type of material, studies showed. Men who watched two movies portraying positive consequences of violence against women seemed to develop increased acceptance of interpersonal violence. Women who saw the same material became less accepting. Sexually violent material can affect the attitudes of sensitive individuals. 25 to 30 percent of men in Malamuth's research showed some tendency to aggress against women.

"We're actually talking about aggressive tendencies that may exist to greater or lesser degree in many so-called normal men," said Dr. Malamuth. That is why the kinds of attitudes that are created are so important.[6]

Sexually violent material can contribute to a social climate in which violence against women is more accepted and thus may be more likely to occur. For some people the distinction between fantasy and reality may not always be very clear, and the group most open to being affected is young people because their sexual patterns aren't yet set. It is a very poor learning experience for them, and it is coming into the home. The concerned Christian parent must stop this invasion!

Penthouse—Hustler—and Others

The amount and vicious character of violence in the mass media is steadily increasing. Magazines such as *Penthouse* and *Hustler* are examples of media that fuse sexually explicit material with violence as are "slasher" films, many of which are only R-rated. In fact, a lot of this material is quite readily available today.

Videocassettes of some of the goriest movies (remember these are rated R, not X), are available for $1 rental at almost any video shop. For many years, those who wanted to view violence had to pay a fee and enter a theater. Now such material is easily accessible to children below the age of discretion via cable TV. The average 10 to 13 year-old watches 100 R-rated films per year or two a week.[7]

The cable television movie channels such as Home Box Office, Showtime, and Cinemax display the Motion Picture Association of America ratings before the showing of films. The viewer is to choose the films to be seen accordingly. What about unsupervised children and teens? Even the most conscientious parent doesn't spend every minute with his child. Cable comes into the home 24 hours per day. The flip of the dial will take a child from the Nickelodeon children's channel to a Cinemax screening of *Porky's II*, an R-rated film recently screened at 7:00 P.M.

The rating system can't always be depended upon for guidance. Through our research we have discovered a couple little "tricks of the trade." First of all, the movie that you see on your pay cable channel or rent from your local video store may not be the same version shown in theaters. A film that was edited to qualify for an R or PG-13 rating often has the questionable scenes of bloody gore restored for release on cable or videocassettes. Neither of these media have the restrictions that networks and theaters do. Therefore, even if you have seen the movie in the theater and found it inoffensive, a parent cannot feel confident that the video his teen wants to rent is the same version.

Another thing that a parent must be aware of in the media is that a movie can be released as "unrated." Contrary to the belief of many of the people to whom we have spoken, these movies are not "safe." As a matter of fact, many producers release movies "unrated" simply because they don't want the stigma of an X attached to them. Since they don't have an R or X rating, even young teens can rent unrated movies.

The Unrated

"This savage alien is on a protein mission. Unfortunately, the vegetarian dinner served up by his two lesbian hosts does not satisfy him. This film contains sexual and cannibalistic scenes . . ." thus is *Alien Prey* described in Video Movie Guide 1988. The "B" section of this guide offers unrated *Best of Sex and Violence* which it says contains "profanity, nudity, and, of course, sex and violence." *Blood Feast* is "crude, vulgar, and ineptly acted . . ." It is also unrated.[8] There are 24 letters of the alphabet left, but we think that you have gotten the idea. Therefore, when the "U" (unrated) classification is announced on your favorite movie channel or the jacket of the video cassette that your teen wants to rent, BEWARE!

A Minister Falls

A beautiful woman is taking a bubble bath in a luxurious setting. Suddenly, she's interrupted by a psychotic killer with some brutal type of weapon who terrorizes her and, ultimately, kills her. Drs. Donnerstein and Linz have studied reactions to the very violent mainly R-rated films like *I Spit on Your Grave, Texas Chainsaw Massacre,* and *Toolbox Murder.* Viewers of such scenes register a connection between sex and violence and begin unconsciously to accept the two as belonging together. They found that, initially, viewers are bothered and depressed by this content. But as they watch more and more of it they not only become desensitized, they begin to find the material enjoyable.[9]

Moody Monthly's article titled "Video Seduction" emphasized that this type of media can attract and corrupt even the most sincere Christian, if we aren't cautious. Here a minister tells of his fall into the depravity of the X-rated movies:

The anonymous author described his initial view of the VCR as a help to his ministry because *Bible* stories, Christian speakers, and seminary courses were available. The minister soon discovered the video shop and began renting Walt Disney classics for his family's viewing. When he heard Christian friends talking about action-adventure movies, he justified watching the less-than-wholesome entertainment by telling himself, "Others are doing it." The author admitted that the longer he watched these films, he found the sexual scenes more enticing and less offensive. He saw no discrepancy when he told his children that they could not watch PG movies "because of bad language and things that were not very nice."

The day soon came when the minister rented an R-rated movie which he admitted attracted him because of the sexually suggestive picture and title. Before long he was watching several movies per week and rationalizing his spiritual struggle by telling himself, "There is nothing wrong with merely viewing these things. I'm not the one doing them." Yet deep within his heart, he knew that he was guilty. The author's effectiveness as a minister suffered—his enthusiasm for teaching and preaching the *Bible* waned and he lost boldness in speaking against immorality. When his wife went to a weekend conference, this Christian pastor rented his first X-rated movie. "It's just curiosity, not lust . . . as a Christian leader, I should be aware of what the world is consuming," he told himself.

What he saw was ugly. The film degraded men and women. At this point, God brought him to his senses. He realized that he was in danger of destroying his life and his ministry. He made a confession to the Lord, his wife, and to a pastor he respected, and vowed to warn other Christians who own video equipment. No person, no matter how spiritual a Christian may consider himself to be, is immune to the temptations of video seduction.[10]

15

Horror On The Big Screen

"Oh, Mom, everyone is going, and Jenny next door has seen it seven times."

How many times have you heard this? For today's youth, like the youth of the 1920's, the "latest," "newest," and "most exciting" film becomes an event to be shared with friends. It is through this sharing that children, teens and adults develop their attitudes of what is "normal." These attitudes are encouraged by acceptance and approval of family and friends. Therefore, when a parent takes a young child or permits a teen to attend a brutally violent or sexually explicit movie, the parent is telling the teen that it is okay to act the way the movie teaches. And, some of today's movies are teaching lessons that no one wants learned! The glorification of brute force and the lack of concern about females are "values" displayed in glamorous formats. Do we really want our adolescents to continually be exposed to films that show drug dealing, robbery, adultery, promiscuity, and murder as acceptable? Do we want to instill in ourselves a lack of sensitivity about pain or death?

Because of their popularity today, some might regard horror films as a strictly modern preoccupation of film makers and moviegoers. In fact, the horror movie genre is nearly as old as the motion picture story itself. Motion pictures were used to tell stories when the first film version of *Dr. Jekyll and Mr. Hyde* was produced in Chicago in 1908. Two years later *Frankenstein* was released. **One**

**authority on horror films believes that a dispropor-
tionate number of horror movies today are not
parables, or stories designed to teach a lesson, as
they were in years past.**

What are horror movies today? Many of the films and
videos researched for this book suggest that they are a
far cry from their early twentieth century predecessors.
**Many of today's movies are bloodbaths, the bloodier
the better. Their paper-thin story lines are steeped
in torturous killings, sexual perversions, and occult
dealings.**

Slasher Films

"I liked the part where the girl chopped off her dad's
head and ate it as a birthday cake," *(Friday the 13th)*
wrote one child when a group of 10 and 11 year-olds were
asked to tell their favorite part from a movie that they
had seen. Some other answers were:

- "I liked it when the alien ate the lady's head and kept on
  burping." *(Xtro)*
- "I liked where they chopped a lady up and all white spurted
  out of her" *(Evil Dead).*
- "I like the bit where the man jumps up and chops off the people's
  hands, fingers, legs, arms and heads."*(Burning)*
- "When the man's weenie got pulled off." *(Blood Beach)*
- "When the rats eat up the baby." *(Rats)*[1]

Aren't these pleasant memories of a family night at the
movies for a 10 year-old?

The graphically violent horror movie is popular today,
largely because of two movies introduced in the late 1960's
and early 1970's: *Night of the Living Dead* and the *Texas
Chainsaw Massacre.* Never before had widely released
films descended to such shocking depths. They showed
human life as nothing more valuable than a slab of meat
to be hacked up, sawed off, or chewed by other living
beings.

Today this kind of motion picture is commonplace, and moviegoers flock to these shock horror movies in droves. In addition to enormous box office success, the slasher movie packed with gratuitous sex and violence is a lucrative video market. Though many movies have adult viewers, the target audience for most of these films is young— preteens, teenagers, and young adults.

Film critics dismiss these pictures as harmless, ridiculous cult films with no socially redeeming value. However, most young people do not bring a sophisticated background in film study to their viewing experience. What they do bring to movies are the attitudes and values they have learned from their parents and in their schools and churches. **Though a child may feel disgust the first time he sees a man eaten alive by a walking dead man, he gradually becomes desensitized to human suffering with each graphically violent act that he sees. Any lessons that he might have learned about the sanctity of human life or about violence in society will ultimately be replaced by a desire to be terrified and to view suffering inflicted on others as entertainment.**

Fear is Entertaining

People like to be scared. Why? There are several reasons. First of all, consider how the body reacts to fear in real life situations. When you are scared, your heart rate increases, your pulse quickens, your senses sharpen, and adrenaline starts pumping through your body. Some people find this agitated state to be a kind of "rush," much like riding a roller coaster. Whether it is caused by a real life situation or by watching a horror movie, fear produces a physical reaction that some people find exhilarating. If a horror movie scares them to a sufficient degree, it was a "good" movie.

Movies have become a popular art form because young and old people get to see their dreams and fantasies come to life on the screen. Shock and horror movies offer very explicit fantasies about subjects that are taboo in real life. Horror movie makers capitalize on one quality unique to humans—the ability to fantasize. Many people's unspoken, sordid fantasies are explored by bringing taboo subjects to the screen: cannibalism, necrophilia, patricide, devil worship, rape, etc.

II Timothy 1:7 reads, *For God hath not given us the spirit of fear; but of power, and of love, and of a sound mind.*

Sad to say, there are those who pay no heed to the Word of God and delight in fear-inducing stimuli. In fact, *some people have a sadistic appetite for fear. They enjoy seeing someone else's fear.* "Why?" you ask. Horror moviegoers will often respond that they can detach themselves from the horror they see because they know that the movie is not real. However, horror movies are sometimes adapted from true life occurrences. The *Texas Chainsaw Massacre,* released in 1974, was based on a true case study of a mass murderer. The movie's leather-faced serial killer was a caricature drawn from Ed Gine, a grave robber who lived in a small isolated Texas town. Ed was a cannibal, a necrophile and a transvestite. He did not dress in women's clothes, however. He dressed in their skin. How can anyone find entertainment value from watching a human's body being sawed up into parts for human consumption, all the while knowing that these crimes were drawn from something that happened in life?

New Video Craze

Teenagers are gathering to watch living creatures die. Statistics on a new kind of video craze suggest that gore itself has entertainment value. These gory videos titled

The Faces of Death are not exculsively occult or pornographic movies, neither are they fiction. These videos peddle real human suffering, with 80 percent of the films taken from newsreels, film libraries and home movies. Violent deaths are clearly depicted in these videos, which although banned in 46 countries, have already sold 160,000 copies in the United States. *The Faces of Death*, wildly popular with teenagers, contain the following footage:

- A man dying during open heart surgery.
- A slaughter house scene showing killings of cows, sheep and a chicken.
- A restaurant scene where guests are seated at a table. The waiter brings out two small hammers and a live monkey, which is forced into a compartment in the table with only its head showing. The patrons proceed to crack open the monkey's skull with their hammers, then eat the brains.
- A gunfight in Los Angeles, in which the police drove a killer out of a house where he had been holding victims. The camera then follows the officers into the house to reveal a woman who had her throat sliced open and two children dead beside her.
- Inmates being put to death in the United States.
- The beheading of a man in Arabia.
- A real life snuff scene done as part of a cult ritual in San Francisco. The dead man, lying on a pentagram, is cut open and his insides are exposed to gain spiritual power to live forever. After eating the man's flesh, the cult had an orgy with the blood of the man rubbed on their body parts. (This subject is also discussed in our book titled *Halloween and Satanism*.)
- Starvation and holocaust scenes.
- A man mauled to death by a grizzly bear.
- A man falling to his death after his parachute did not open.
- The remains of a woman, who had been riding a bicycle when she was hit by a semi-truck.

Somehow, the distinction between reality and fantasy has become so blurred that teenagers are flocking to video stores to see not special effects, but real living creatures dying. We can't think of anything more sadistic. *The Faces of Death* uses some of the most brutal human and animal scenes of death and killing imaginable as a means of entertainment.

The films conclude with a simple teaching on reincarnation, which very handily suggests that human life is dispensible. While the death of our mortal bodies is inevitable, cruel and ususual human suffering is not an inevitable or necessary part of life, and it certainly should not be packaged as entertainment.

Attraction and Inspiration

"Watch over 100 violent acts every half hour." "View scenes of brutal torture." Is it this type of invitation that is the attraction of violence and horror? Is it the scantily-clad females pictured in the ads? Whatever the lure, people are flocking to films high in violence and horror in huge numbers. Consequently, these movies are grossing large amounts of money.

***Rambo* had groups of people terminated in over 70 explosions, and 44 specific killings for an average of one death for every 2.1 minutes of the 93 minute film. *Commando* grossed $100 million—or about one dollar for every guy the Schwarzenegger character blew away. *Predator* grossed $107 million, and *The Running Man* made $10.5 million its first week.**[2]

Non-stop violence in movies such as *Indiana Jones and The Temple of Doom* earned more than $165,000,000. *Alien Prey* features a blood-stained vampire who feasts on a dead woman's entrails through a hole in her stomach. *Make Them Die Slowly* proudly proclaims "24 SCENES OF BARBARIC TORTURE," including a scene in which a man slices a woman in half. *Flesh Feast* reveals "body maggots" that consume live human beings, pulling the skin off the victims' faces before working their way down.

Your home is no longer a haven safe from savage violence and inhumanity. It is surprising to see how heavy the consumption of brutal modern monster movies is even in Christian homes. At one Catholic high school 75 percent of the student body had seen *Friday the 13th* and 20 percent had seen *Texas Chainsaw Massacre*.[3] Typically, films like these are reported to have been seen at home on pay television stations. Innocent children are viewing an enormous number of intensely sadistic and violent videos at home that they could not see in public theaters.

Is this disgusting entertainment affecting the viewers? As with television programs and films, some movies inspire imitation:

A 13 year-old shot William Hammond, age 3, in the head with a .22 caliber bullet after watching *The Outlaw Josie Wales* starring Clint Eastwood. The teen got his father's pistol from the bedroom and fired it at the visiting youngster. The investigating detective concluded that the movie had played a role in causing the shooting.[4]

After a five-year-old Boston boy allegedly stabbed a two-year-old girl, he told police that he was inspired by the horror movies that had recently appeared on television. Police said that after the attack, the boy and this three-year-old cousin who was present at the stabbing, talked about the characters Freddie of *Nightmare On Elm Street* and Jason of *Friday The 13th*. The youngster had used a kitchen knife to repeatedly stab the 2 year-old in the hips and thighs. She received stitches in nine of the wounds.

Kimberly Goytia, a 13 year-old from Sacramento, murdered her 11 year-old sister due to direct influence of the movie *The Omen*. The district attorney said that Kimberly had worshipped the devil since seeing the movie.[5]

These are but a small fraction of the deaths related to the use of horror and violence for entertainment. By far the most famous of the copycats is the unprecedented number of deaths following the movie *Deerhunter*. One scene in the movie pictures American prisoners in Vietnam being forced to play Russian roulette. In this "game of chance" all chambers of a pistol are empty except one. The player puts the pistol to his head and (not knowing which chamber hold the bullet) pulls the trigger. The movie was broadcast on HBO, and by April 1984, 35 Russian roulette shootings had been reported. There had been 31 deaths, all male, half of them under age 18. By January 1986, the number had risen to 41 deaths. It is interesting to note that the vast majority of these deaths followed the HBO presentation of *Deerhunter* on cable television rather than its theatrical release.

The Occult and Horror

Today's horror movies delve heavily into the occult. One obvious reason is that as the viewing public's appetite increases, it needs to be served more evil and heinous crimes than in the previous movie to get the same "rush." For example, when Boris Karloff first appeared as Dr. Frankenstein's monster, a creature made from corpses dug up from the cemetery and brought to life, moviegoers were horror-stricken. Today, Frankenstein's image hardly scares anyone. In fact, it even adorns a box of children's cereal.

Evil humans and supernatural villains derive their powers from serving the prince of darkness in horror pictures. Many twisted crimes are committed by humans on other humans in real life. However, movie makers found that by using monsters who were plucked from the "nether world," inspired or controlled by the devil, they could commit crimes with far more shock value. Sometimes the evil character's connection to the devil is implied, as in *Halloween*. In this picture, the stalking murderer springs back into life after assaults that would kill any normal human being. Other times the connection to Satan is deliberate. For instance, in *Cathy's Curse,* a demon enters a woman's womb to impregnate her (there is more about this subject in *Halloween and Satanism*).

Occult horror movies have high entertainment value because they combine frightful violence, sex, and taboo subjects such as devil worship all in one picture. After all, those who worship Satan would have the most evil natures and relentlessly carnal appetites of all human beings. Sensational story lines have been written about lawless humans, indulging in the flesh, satisfying every base appetite imaginable. What follows is a short list of occult horror films, and a sampling of scenes from them:

Eerie Midnight Horror Show
This occult-based movie shows a woman being crucified, her hands and feet nailed to a cross. It is blatantly anti-Christian.
Madhouse Mansion
Demonism, witchcraft, beatings and stabbings make up the brunt of this picture.
To Devil A Daughter
A pregnant woman about to be delivered is tied to a bed, with her legs and feet tied together so that she dies trying to give birth.
Vampyres
This movie contains overtly sexual scenes, lesbianism, cannibalism and orgies.

Poltergeist, The Exorcist, Rosemary's Baby, and *The Omen* are all movies made popular because of the current fascination with the occult. Don't close your eyes to the effects that these movies have on those who watch them, especially children.

Horror movies will continue to vary in their shock value and their graphically, violent, sexual and occult content.

Just because some of these movies are big box office hits, it is dangerous to assume that they are harmless and their content is socially acceptable. Consider what behaviors the movie is condoning: casual sex, dabbling with the occult for recreation, or graphic violence and needless human suffering. Think of what the effects might be of repeated exposure to these kinds of films.

Perhaps adults can see through some of the schemes movie makers use to trump up the entertainment value of a movie. Maybe they are even aware of the techniques used to manipulate their feelings and passions. Simply because they are older and sometimes wiser, adults are not immune to the desensitizing effects of horror movies. The triple X-rated horror flicks are made to tempt and demoralize adult audiences. Many of the occult films make a mockery of Christianity.

However, the target audience for the most of the slasher movies is not adults; it is young people. Young people are targeted at a time when they may just becoming oriented with their changing bodies and their increased feelings for the opposite sex. What happens to the young people whose first exposure to sex is molestation and violent fornication as seen on the screen? They may not even have any knowledge of the opposite sex as expression of love to temper the impact of seeing violent sex. What happens to children who learn to cultivate an appetite for human suffering, or who enjoy seeing women made into victims time and time again? Because they often lack an adult's guidance and perspective, children are at the mercy of the filmmakers. We can only guess what the long-range effects might be: that some children will be more deeply affected than others; that attitudes about caring, loving relationships might be eclipsed for years by desires to satisfy appetites of the flesh; that a whole generation of Americans may grow up with relative indifference to the suffering of living creatures. Considering the many challenges and temptations children face today, what price will be paid if we don't use discretion choosing the films that we watch, and that they watch?

16

MTV And Video Games

. . I will sing with the spirit, and I will sing with the understanding also. . . I Cor. 14:15

The newest member of the violent TV family is just a kid, relatively speaking, but don't let its age fool you. This "kid's" daily appearance in 27 million homes has helped the record industry realize profits soaring into billions of dollars in the 1980's. It is an entertainment sensation—a slick, sophisticated marriage of rock music and film called MTV.

Since its introduction into popular culture in the 50's, rock and roll has captured the teenage audience. Many parents did not want to listen to it then, and still don't want their children listening to it, perhaps with good reason. The fact that many parents continue to be intolerant of popular music has not changed much in more than thirty years, but a lot of other things have changed.

The Dark Side of MTV

These days rock and roll's influence is greater than ever. You find punk rock, heavy metal, acid rock, and rap everywhere, but have you ever truly listened to this rude, crude elevator music of the younger generation? Suffering from a lack of real musical creativity, but still anxious to haul in the billion dollar profits, the mainstream music industry today peddles more raunchy records and videos than ever. The buyers are getting younger and younger with ten to twenty-four-year olds buying 64 percent of the records and tapes sold in the United States. **Studies show that before today's teenagers graduate from high school, they will have listened to 10,500 hours of rock music. That is only 500 hours less than the total time they will have spent in school over a 12 year period.**[1] The music industry is big business, and MTV is big business to anyone in the music industry. If you want to sell a record in today's competitive market, you have to make a video.

"I Want My MTV"

More people watch music videos than tune in to the CBS evening news. MTV is ranked sixth among cable systems in the United States, and its programs have a daily audience of 21.5 million. *One fourth of the music video viewing audience is under age 15.* If all videos were as socially conscious as "We Are the World" (theme song for Live-Aid) or as benign as "All Night Long" (by Lionel Richie), the only problem with MTV might be that kids are spending too much time being "couch potatoes" when they should be doing other things.

The truth is that 30 percent of music videos aired between 1986 and 1987 contained explicitly violent themes or lyrics. *Without any warning to young viewers, a typical hour of MTV programming mixes violent or sexually explicit videos with nonviolent videos as casually as a floral arrangement mixes silk flowers with dried herbs.* Those who program MTV admit that they are indiscriminate. "We play basically everything that is give to us . . . We're like an art gallery. We just put the paintings on the wall," says one executive.[2] As a consequence, millions of children and teenagers are exposed to rock videos masquerading as pop "art" that are often sadomaschistic explorations into devil worship and erotica.

The Dangerous Lure of Music Video

Rock lyrics might have been difficult to understand in the past, since rock artists alternately scream and mumble the words. But, thanks to the music video, the message of the music is no longer an exercise in guesswork. It becomes explicit. If children are too young to know what certain words mean, they are quickly educated through rhythmic film editing that leaves nothing to the imagination. Videos make strong impressions on young viewers whose attention spans are short.

"Pop music is creating false puberty among kids," says Peter Christenson, assistant professor of communications at Lewis and Clark College.[3] Many music videos now airing combine obscene lyrics, violence, and exploitation of women in a repetitive format that needs careful monitoring. Children of all ages are drawn to lurid songs and videos, and psychologists are afraid of the consequences of saturating kids with sex and violence at such an early age.

Thanks to MTV, many previously unknown pop rock singers are not only household names but are trend setters. As purveyors of modern culture, they influence not only what kids wear or how they style their hair, but also how they behave. Music videos have a tremendous impact on children because they are like a fan magazine come to life, showcasing favorite rock stars and teen idols. Because they lack exposure to better heroes, many kids idolize these heart throbs gyrating around on our big picture TVs. **Music videos are more likely to have greater effects on children's social behavior than are regular TV shows.**

Those effects can't be desirable when many artists and rock groups go to any extreme to be antisocial and downright obscene. Rock star Alice Cooper was one of the early proponents of "shock rock." He used guillotines and giant boa constrictor snakes to terrify and excite the audience. The band Kiss elaborated on Cooper's theatrical violence and drew nationwide protests and fans. They were the first to use grotesque makeup and outrageous costumes. Ozzy Osbourne horrified rock fans by biting off the head of a live bat during one performance. W.A.S.P. is a heavy metal band whose name stands for "We Are Sexual Perverts." This group brags that they have tied women on a rack during shows and pretended to cut their throats. Many of the heavy metal bands are in a competition to be considered the most gross and violent. The group Venom brags about how much it knows about rituals of devil worship and reportedly "espouses every negative quality known to mankind." Iron Maiden has a mascot named Eddie. At every one of their performances, the group rips out Eddie's brain and throws it to the audience.

Violent and Lurid Images

Some of the rock bands that desire air time on MTV have had to reduce the violence in their videos. However, the level of violence that MTV finds acceptable is extreme, as is shown by the Car's music video *You Might Think*. In this video, a monster carries a woman away, uses a jackhammer to drill her tooth, climbs a building with the woman in tow and drops her from the roof. The monster runs over her with a car, and her head pops off.

If actions speak louder than words, then sadomasochistic videos speak volumes to young people about sex and violence, perhaps before they are old enough to understand about sex and love. That is because these erotically violent acts aren't performed by antiheroes, but by stars that are idolized. In the video *Photograph* by Def Leppard, a character known as the "Passion Killer" kisses and kills Marilyn Monroe. It shows scantily clad women in cages and a dead woman tied with wire. The video *Women* by the same group is a montage of comic book scenes about a planet of women produced for man's pleasure and to serve him. One of the violent acts includes a woman hanging by her arms from the ceiling. Such portrayals of women suggest to young people that women need to be sexual to have any power at all.

When you are watching MTV, you are learning that it is nice to hang women by the wrists and beat them up while you sing. Motley Crue's *Looks That Kill* involves women in cages being attacked by the studded-leather-clad male band. A laser-shooting woman frees them and sets the band on fire. Billy Idol's *Dancing With Myself* shows the star using electricity to blow people off a building. A man sharpens a straight-edge razor as if to kill a naked woman, chained behind a translucent sheet. A man with a hammer sneaks up on a woman to kill her. One half of the women in videos are provocatively dressed. **Young girls who watch a lot of MTV pick up the message that they've got to project themselves sexually to get attention from boys. Meanwhile the boys are learning that women are important only for their sexual entertainment value.**

Other lurid images in videos include a rape scene in a gay bar portrayed by Frankie Goes to Hollywood. One Duran Duran video simulates a sexual encounter between two women. Judas Priest describes oral sex forced at gun point in *Eat Me Alive*. And, Prince pays tribute to incest in his song *Sister*.

"If you are a non-white in a video, you are there to blow someone up or be blown up," adds researcher Barry Sherman.[4]

In addition to being sexest, the message of many music videos is also racist. Blacks, hispanics, and Asians are more likely to be victims of violence than are whites. Like women, non-whites are more often depicted as subservient to white males.

The After-Effects

We're possessed by all that is evil
The death of you, God, we demand
We spit at the virgin you worship
And sit at Lord Satan's left hand

from the album *Welcome To Hell* by Venom[5]

On the average, every half hour of music videos contains 18 violent acts. The after-effects are tragic for more than a few teenagers: Friends of Richard Ramirez, the "Night Stalker" charged with 16 murders on the West Coast said that Ramirez was obsessed with the satanic message of *Highway to Hell*, an album put out by the heavy metal band AC/DC. Ramirez painted satanic pentagrams on the walls of some of the victims. A 14 year-old-girl, also obsessed with heavy metal music was sentenced to 25 years in prison for stabbing and bludgeoning her mother to death. A video put out by Twisted Sister reportedly led to a copycat murder in New Mexico in 1984. Dr. Paul King, medical director of the adolescent program at Charter Lakeside Hospital, a psychiatric and addictive disease facility in Memphis, Tennessee, says that over 80 percent of the adolescent patients he treats have listened to heavy metal music for several hours a day. Dr. King notes that 50 percent of them know the words to the songs and can write them down. He states, ". . . the lyrics become a philosophy of life, a religion."[6]

Less tragic, but more widespread is the finding that heavy viewing of music videos can increase levels of depression and anxiety, especially in female viewers. Dr.

Radecki sees young people with anger and antisocial behavior problems in his psychiatric practice. These young people are steeped in "sub-culture" created by violent rock music. Radecki says it is "plainly obvious that they are heavily immersed in fantasies of violence (which) is affecting their way of thinking and their behavior in an anti-social direction."[7]

What Can Be Done?

What price are children going to pay to learn right and wrong? Are they going to pay with their mental stability or their virginity, by contracting a sexually transmitted disease, by delving into devil worship, or by serving a jail sentence? Joan Ganz Cooney, president of Children's Television Workshop believes that entertainment that glorifies violence may be like throwing a match on gasoline. Why are we so complacent as a society about these antisocial messages?

Childhood innocence is under siege by the entertainment industry. Movies, TV, home videos, and music videos are more violent and explicitly sexual than ever before. The easiest course would be to jump ship, wait for others to clean up the airwaves, or wait until artists and programming executives accept the responsibility and take action.

Though legislators and political groups are trying to move Congress to enact legislation requiring that record albums be rated according to sexual and violent content, it may be a long time before this happens. Equal numbers of prominent politicians oppose censorship of any kind. Artists are crying that censorship denies them their Constitutional right to free speech, and not to deaf ears.

In the meantime, what can parents do to protect their children from the adverse effects of video sex and violence? Don't turn your head to the things your children are watching. Pay attention to what they are seeing and hearing on music videos. If something they have seen is upsetting to you or them, talk with them. Give them a framework of values, so that they don't place undue importance on the bad things they see and hear on TV. Best of all, help guide them into plenty of activities, so that they have more constructive things to do with their time than turn on the TV set. Teach them as the *Bible* counsels: *have no fellowship with the unfruitful works of darkness, but rather reprove them.* Ephesians 5:11

Violent Video Games

As if a heavy diet of violence in televised cartoons, prime time programming, sports and movies was not enough, America's insatiable appetite for violence has found yet another taste sensation—violent video games. Though they only run on pocket change, arcade games are a more profitable enterprise than Hollywood movies. One of the nation's leading manufacturers in the multibillion dollar video game industry, Atari spends $125 million on advertising their games, and another $25 million on research to produce best-selling games.[8]

Practicing to be Violent

". . . thefts and assaults . . . nearly 300 arrests . . ." reads a passage from a news story out of Japan. Is it the report of a riot or the after-effects of a natural disaster? No, the television reports concern the day the video game Dragon's Quest III was released for sale. More than one million copies of this computer game were sold that single day. Japanese authorities reported thefts and assaults along the extensive lines of people waiting to make their purchase as well as nearly 300 arrests for truancy among school kids cutting classes to get their hands on the ($45) game.[9]

The Japanese are not the only ones who have developed an avid interest in video games. The instant popularity of this form of amusement in the United States is due to America's love of television. We have grown accustomed to sitting in front of a screen for entertainment, and playing games through the TV is the next logical step. In fact, one study suggests that because of their fast pace, youngsters prefer video games to watching television. To heavy video game players, TV becomes "boring."

"In TV, if you want to make someone die, you can't. In Pac-Man, if you want to run into a ghost you can; On TV you can't say 'shoot now' or, with Popeye, 'eat your spinach now'."[10] These were some of the comments of children ages 8 through 14 when asked to explain their preference for video games. One youngster further explained that she would get frustrated while watching Popeye, because he wouldn't eat his spinach when she wanted him to. Since children have such great control over the video games they play, these games afford them a false sense of omnipotence. They come to believe that all their thoughts and actions are complete, perfect and without challenge. This is certainly not a Christian attitude!

So, **at a time in their lives when children should be learning how to control their impulses and that they can't have everything exactly the way that they would like it to be, they are instead acquiring a taste for total control and immediate gratification through playing video games.** In addition, research shows actual participation in violence is a more powerful teacher than viewing it on the screen. In essence, our children are practicing to be violent when they play violent video games. "These video games will become so real that (they) will have trouble distinguishing between what is real and what isn't," says one video game designer.[11]

Even non-violent video games are flawed in the same way as their electronic predecessor—the TV. Just as TV watching is an activity of isolation, video game playing does not encourage social interaction. Playing games in an arcade is hardly a social activity, even if there are many others around. Players all stand with their backs to one another in a room very dimly lit to enhance the images on the screens. Video game players have the same vacant look in their eyes as heavy television viewers, as they madly maneuver joysticks and buttons in competitions against themselves.

Playing a solitary video game, such as Space Invaders, may stimulate further aggression in the player, and most home and arcade games are one-person games. A study involving the two-person game, video boxing, found that playing a video game with another actually may reduce levels of aggression. This is particularly true if one player can't beat the machine without the cooperation of the other player.

Violent Games People Play

That children play violent games is not a 1980's phenomenon. Many army games as well as cowboy and Indian battles have been acted out in the past, perhaps even in your own past. However, it seems that the majority of the games that are manufactured for children today are based on violent themes and use violent actions. The NCTV found 90 percent of arcade video games and 85 percent of home video games to be violent.

The destruction of others is the core of these games. Following an afternoon of killing off hundreds, perhaps thousands, of Space Invaders, children no longer have any genuine feelings about taking the life of another. One child remarked, "Why should I care about the enemy? The point is to kill them."[12]

"There's an awful lot of potential violence and destruction of imagined enemies in playing these video games. This promotes an aggressive attitude on the part of the child. The games strengthen aggressive tendencies and that is fundamentally wrong," says Dr. Alex Skavenski, professor of psychology at Northeastern University.[13]

Some of the games are violent forays into fantasy and science fiction worlds, and some are so frighteningly realistic that they could be viewed as military training exercises. We were distressed to find that there are even sexually violent video games available which are quite popular with adults. Here are some of the violent video games being marketed today:

Beserk
Encourages the player to simulate shooting as many people as he or she can in a shooting rampage. The game programs the machine to call the player "Chicken" if it does not shoot people quickly enough.

Utopia
Lets the player be a dictator, fighting rebels.

F-15 Strike Eagle
A flight simulator program which includes "Mission 8: The Anti-Terrorist Airstrike—Libya," complete with a printed map of the coastline of Libya dotted with suspected terrorist camps, and F-15's.

Space Ace
A clean-cut white young American male who blasts away the bad guys with a handgun and gains young females as his reward for doing so.

River Raid
The player is at the controls of a B1 bomber, with enemy jets, helicopters and ships as targets.

Custer's Revenge
A game that uses rape.

Beat 'Em and Eat 'Em
Featuring a man on a rooftop who ejaculates into the mouths of two women below.

There are a myriad of other games on the market, with lots of companies currently competing for that fat video game dollar.

Elimate, Kill, Destroy

When I'm depressed and angry about something that happened at school, I can come here and shoot away rather than blowing up my history teacher," one boy confesses.[14]

People are beginning to understand "the adverse mental and physical effects of video games on children . . . They are into it body and soul. Their body language is tremendous and everything is zap the enemy. Martians are coming in that have to be killed, the enemy is coming here (and) you have to zap them. Everything is eliminate, kill, destroy, let's get up and do it fast," comments Surgeon General Koop.[15] He and many other experts believe that violent electronic games make children more accepting of real violence and more inclined to use it. Violent video games encourage distorted feelings of power and control in players, and do not encourage children to cultivate patience.

Just as TV programmers are convinced that viewers want violent programs, video game manufacturers believe consumers want to purchase violent video games. However, as researchers are discovering with TV programming, a video game does not have to be violent to be popular. A perfect example of this is Petball, which is not violent in the least. In fact, some people shy away from the violence in arcade games. This is particularly true of females. Aggressive fantasies may interest men and boys, but are a turn-off for many women and girls. Since video games represent their first exposure to computers, it follows that girls who dislike the violent fantasy computer games may be discouraged from studying and working with computers in general. This is a rapidly expanding field, offering many opportunities for women, provided that they don't develop a bias against computers caused by early exposure to violent video games.

There are alternatives to violent video games on the market today. Some of these include mechanical and historical simulations, designed not to educate, but to entertain. These games are not like any video arcade conterparts with similar sounding names. For example, Flight Simulator II has carefully researched the recreation of a single engine, 148 mph, fixed landing gear aircraft. *Creative Computing* reports that it is the closest thing to flying on a microcomputer. One who plays Space Shuttle attempts to fly a shuttle in true simulation form through launches, rendezvous and docks with satellites, all the while conserving enough fuel to return to earth. Video game manufacturers can use action themes in games, without being violent, and still turn a profit. An action game without violence might include rescuing someone from danger, using quick and original thinking skills.

A Message to Manufacturers

America's schools have become major consumers of computer hardware and software. Many people see computers as a boon to American education as the nation's schools struggle to rise above a state of mediocrity. Educational software represents a virtual frontier of opportunity for manufacturers, as school districts scramble to buy the best. There is a very blatant need for educational software that is imaginative and adequate to teachers' needs.

Rather than spend millions researching, developing and advertising slick, violent video game fantasies or pornographic video games, why not channel some of that enterprise and capital toward improving educational software to serve as a useful supplement for creative teaching? Enough evidence has been collected to suggest that playing violent video games and playing too many video games can have adverse effects on children and adults. Children who play aggressive video games are less likely to come to the aid of others. They cultivate self-centered attitudes, fostered by their solitary competition with the game and themselves.

We all need a variety of activities to fill our leisure time, but none of us needs any more exposure to media violence. Whether video games are purely violent in theme or not, a steady diet of them can lead to creative, social, compassionate, and intellectual malnutrition.

17

TV Sports Violence

Gladiators fought to the death as far back as 264 BC, and some form of sporting competition has been with us ever since. However, the discovery of television as a showcase has brought more and seemingly unnecessary violence into the sports arena.

Professional sports have always been rough, but violence seldom erupted at a sporting event. An isolated incident was not unusual, but was not the "norm" either. Today, individual and team violence is common in most sports. After all, it makes "good television"—sports that are televised seem to have increased in violence simply to attract viewers. Players have been encouraged to fight with, belittle, and in other ways persecute their opponents.

We have seen football players exchange blows after the ball is dead and baseball players lunge in anger at a pitcher who may or may not have hit their batter deliberately with the ball. In 1982, a Los Angeles hockey player was kicked off the team and sent to the minor leagues for refusing to fight at the coach's command.

Not So Quotable Quotes

We hear boxers, football players, and professional wrestlers say things like, "I'm going to make that guy suffer in the ring today; We're going to rough those guys up; We're going to hit them so hard they won't be able to see straight." These kinds of statements attract media attention because they represent pre-game hype which may attract more viewers. Just previous to the 1984 Superbowl, the media gave tremendous attention to intimidation in sports violence, stressing that the Los Angeles Raiders had a reputation for playing "dirty." One Associated Press release quoted the Raiders general manager, Al David as saying, "We like to get in a street fight."[1] Enroute to the Superbowl, the Raiders were accused of provoking fights by pushing and shoving between plays to get their opponents' minds off the game. Raiders' coach Tom Flores responded to the accusations by saying, "We wear black and we do things our own way."[2] That way seems to be close to that described as undesirable in Galatians 5:20-21: *Hostilities, bickering, jealousy, outbursts of rage . . . I warn you, as I have warned you before: those who do such things will not inherit the kingdom of God!*

Violence in the Game

In major league baseball, physical roughness and fights are common. This is supposedly a non-contact sport, yet many players sustain injuries that take them out of action for long periods of time. In professional basketball, roughness and technical fouls have become such a standard of behavior that for a game to be considered successful, the coach must shout, argue, get into a pushing match with the referee, or show some other form of extreme behavior such as throwing chairs.

The violence in football speaks for itself. Incidents where one player has deliberately injured another are common. We have seen tragedies on the playing field. For instance, in 1978 Darryl Stingley, a wide receiver for the New England Patriots was tackled so viciously by Jack Tatum that Stingley suffered a dislocated spine. Tatum, who is nicknamed "The Assassin," is reported to have purposely belted Stingley in the head with his forearm. No penalty was ever called on the play which immediately paralyzed Stingley and ended his football career and his ability to walk.

The biggest problem with the media where sports is concerned is that it doesn't stop at simply reporting violent occurrences. To entice and satisfy the viewer/listener/reader, the media glamorizes the brutality. Fans, young and old alike, get many opportunities to witness incidents of inhumanity thanks to instant replays, zoom lenses, and magazine essays.

Football scuffles, baseball brawls, hockey fistfights and basketball square-offs—acts of passion that go beyond the rules—are a minor part of any sports event. Yet, they are given long and detailed attention and instant and nonstop replay. Commentators are five times more likely to make positive comments about rough play and unnecessary violence during a game than to make negative comments about harmful aggression toward other players. The players most often quoted by broadcasters and sports writers are the ones who make threats against the opposing team.

Newscasts, sports recaps, and newspaper headlines emphasize any and all brutal incidents to delight their audiences. And, the sports fans are being affected. Spectators at sporting events have themselves become violent. It is not uncommon for referees, umpires, or players to be injured by fans, or to need security guard escorts to return to the locker room. At least ten studies show that violent sports frequently increase angry, hostile feelings in viewers and participants.

Role of TV

Just as the use of violence has increased in TV shows and movies, so has the exaggerated use of and attention to violence in sports increased. The reason for this is largely

economic. Unlike the print media, television commentators and broadcasters must use a lot of show business
techniques to hold the audience's attention. According
to sportswriter Leonard Koppett, "Holding attention is
the key economic need . . . So, broadcasters have to
convince their audience to stay tuned in now, for the
duration of the show. Hyperbole and artificial excitement
help do this."[3] If commentators project to the viewing
audience that the game they are watching is anything less
than terrifically exciting and a "can't miss" proposition,
the network will lose present viewers and risks losing future
audiences.

The Spillover Effects

The violence in legitimate sports such as hockey and
boxing continues to be glamorized on television. The
effects of viewing these sports seem to spill over into real
life situations for several days after these games are
televised. Whenever the Boston Bruins are seen on TV,
increased levels of violence are reported in Boston area
youth hockey leagues for several days. A few professional
hockey players, who asked to remain anonymous, said
that they are encouraged by their team owners to be
violent.[4] Here players have attacked each other with such
brutality that some have been charged with criminal
assault. Apparently, team owners have found that a more
violent game increases attendance which leads to bigger
profits. Brawls will continue in the NHL as long as fighting
is viewed as a way of attracting a bigger hockey audience.

Professional Boxing

More than any other violent sport, professional boxing
has come under siege by growing numbers of prominent
organizations. The World Medical Association, the
American Academy of Pediatrics, and the American

Academy of Neurology, among others, have all called for a ban on boxing. At least 13 studies have looked at the impact of boxing on the viewers. All have found an increase in anger and the tendency toward physical violence in viewers, including an increase in homicides in the United States following heavily publicized heavyweight bouts.[5]

An overwhelming amount of medical research proves that boxing causes chronic irreversible brain damage. In addition to the punch drunk syndrome, which is typified by mental confusion, leg dragging, tremors, staggering and impaired speech, professional boxers have suffered dementia, intellectual deterioration, and severe personality disorders. Several professional boxers have died from brain injuries suffered during matches.

Professional boxing could be less dangerous if the number of required rounds in a bout were reduced from 15 to 6, if blows to the head would be disqualified, or if boxers fought without gloves. (When boxing gloves absorb perspiration, they become like clubs, capable of delivering heavier blows.) However, it is not likely that any of these changes would take place because fans, promoters and boxers themselves would reject them. Any of these precautions would make the sport less dangerous and therefore less exciting.

Increasing numbers of physicians are calling for a ban on boxing not only for medical reasons, but for moral reasons. Some experts feel that it is morally wrong for one human being to attempt to deliberately injure the brain of another human being. The surest way to a victory in boxing is to damage the other boxer's brain.

Although the brain damage to the boxers themselves is a tragedy and a national scandal, the research clearly indicates that the greatest damage is to the millions of viewers and to their families and acquaintances. The evidence is clear that televised boxing is causing thousands of beatings and dozens of deaths each year in our country.

Hulk Hogan and Mr. T: Hero or Holligan?

While violence in boxing, hockey and football continues to be glamorized, the worst and most trendy offender is professional wrestling. This cosmos is littered with flamboyant, beefy stars who receive as much air time outside of the wrestling match as during it. Names like Hulk Hogan, Rowdy Roddy Piper, and Sergeant Slaughter have become household words, thanks to heavy media attention. Pro wrestlers get in front of the camera to say how much they hate each other, and brag about how they intend to hurt their opponents. Of course, the fact that Hulk Hogan fights as dirty as an underworld thug is "okay" because he is supposedly a good guy. Even though pro wrestling matches are staged and not real contests, serious consequences are not unknown. Big Daddy Splashdown, a professional wrestler in England, accidentally killed his opponent King Kong Kurt in August of 1987 when he took a flying leap and landed on Kurt. Kurt was instantly killed. Splashdown was back in the ring the next day performing the exact same maneuver on yet another opponent.

The media is whetting the public's appetite for brutality as entertainment by televising these events. Thousands attend pro wrestling matches and millions more tune in through several networks because they enjoy watching brutal slams and kicks, screaming for revenge and yelling for more violence. Such a clamoring does not seem very far removed from the barbaric days of ancient gladiator contests.

Pro wrestlers are clearly portrayed as good or evil personalities, with some of the most hateful hailing from countries like Russia, Iran, and Japan. Regardless of whether the wrestler is perceived as good or bad, they all use violent and illegal tactics such as kicks to the face, choking, eye gouging, hitting with chairs, elbows to the neck, and attempts to maim. The announcers repeatedly emphasize painful holds and lavishly praise the mean and vengeful actions of the wrestlers.

Mr. T and a host of other celebrities including Cyndi Lauper, Dick Clark, Liberace, Gloria Steinem and Geraldine Ferraro have done promotions for professional wrestling. Mr. T has already teamed up with Hogan to fight a widely publicized match against Roddy Piper. Even First Lady Nancy Reagan does not appear to be well-informed on the adverse effects of promoting violent TV characters. She invited Mr. T, pro-wrestler and star of *The A-Team*, the most violent show on TV at the time, to the White House and gave him a kiss on the forehead. Even more alarming about Mr. T's involvement with pro wrestling is that he is reportedly a Christian minister.

Dr. Radecki believes that Mr. T is not aware of the harm his affiliation with pro wrestling has on millions of children and adult viewers. The pro wrestling message is "not a message of self-control, love and understanding. It is a message of seeing your enemy as something less than human and deserving of hatred. It is an exercise in revenge. It is how scientific research has found that violence is taught . . .(Mr. T's) message is the exact opposite of the message of Jesus Christ. Pro wrestling teaches a hatred of your opponent. Instead of trying to convert your enemy, it teaches you to torture him."[6] In defense of this involvement with pro wrestling, Mr. T has claimed that the sport provides a release for aggression. However, research has shown the opposite—that watching pro wrestling increases viewers tendencies toward violence.

Are Today's Athletes Good Role Models?

Youngsters are the most pure and impressionable of all sports fans. They are intensely loyal to their favorite teams and easily captivated as spectators. Those who become hooked on sports as children are likely to be addicted to sports for the rest of their lives. Sports events promoters are keenly aware of the young fans. After all, " . . . children who root grow up to be adults who buy," as one renown sports writer said.[7] As a result children are plied with promotional items such as pennants, caps, cups and T-shirts. Local stores are filled with sportswear emblazoned with the names of mascots or favorite teams.

On top of all these promotional items geared at snaring young fans is the simple reality that when kids play baseball, football, basketball, and wrestle "just like the guys on TV," they often imagine themselves as their favorite sports heroes catching that line drive or slam-dunking the ball through the hoop. Children like to imitate and like to pretend, and they do so with ease.

Athletes have always been regarded as role models for children. In past eras, athletes' less than squeaky clean exploits and bad habits were carefully guarded from the public. Whether today's athletes are into more illicit activities such as drug use and gambling than were previous generations of athletes is a matter of opinion. However, it is certain that everything athletes do today, good and bad, makes a big splash in the media. If an athlete has a cocaine problem, America knows about it. If he has used steroids, we know that, too. Sports page headlines tell us of heroes who announce their engagement to one woman and the birth of a child to another while joking that a divorce from a third is "pending." "Ballplayer arrested again" headlines keep the sports fan informed of the antics of his favorite teams. Meanwhile, our young fans are absorbing all of this. There is a significant effect on children when they find out the ball player that they pretend to be in the backyard, the one they most idolize, is going to jail for drug trafficking.

It is also irresponsible for athletes to appear on TV and in magazines to sell beer and tobacco. Children get the message from the media that to excel in sports one must drink beer, chew tobacco, do drugs, and punch everyone within range.

As more and more athletes appear in commercials, on talk shows, and in interviews, their influence as role models continues to grow. The difference today is that children have two sides of sports stars to imitate—the player as an athlete and the player as a personality.

Nice Guys Finish Last

This is a lesson that American children learn early in life, perhaps even during their first game of musical chairs. When the music stops, preschool children all scramble to the remaining chairs so as not to feel the humiliation of being left standing when all the other children are seated. Nice guys don't win in musical chairs. The children who win are the ones who quickly learn that winning means being able to take for themselves, and to push others out of the way, even if it means that someone might get hurt.

Thus, at very young ages children learn that it takes being mean to win at a game. This concept is reinforced by watching sports events on television and following the lives of favorite sports heroes in the media. Boys don't learn that it is okay to be aggressive just within the sport. The competitive, unfriendly behaviors kids learn often spill over into non-sports situations. "After a steady diet of the killer instinct message from age eight through sixteen, it would seem that the boys could only escalate to machine gunning the opposition high school, atom bombing Notre Dame and hydrogen bombing the Dallas Cowboys," says one expert.[8]

"Winning isn't everything. It's the only thing."[9] Sports commentator Howard Cosell claims that this principle did not always apply to sports in America, but it does now. Winning has become paramount in all sports—at all levels.

This undue emphasis on winning has not resulted in lower calibre sporting events. If anything, athletes get stronger and bigger, run faster, jump higher and farther and break more records with each passing year. So what's missing from sports in America today? How about a sense of goodness and wholesomeness. Sports, at its best, provides a healthy release from hard work or study, the chance for a good workout, and feelings of accomplishment for athletes. If sports can no longer offer these benefits, they have lost the lion's share of their value.

When winning is the most important outcome to those playing, watching or coaching a sporting event, the spirit of the game is lost. It is definitely wrong for a player to try to hurt another player. Parents should encourage good, clean, hard-hitting behavior, if that is what is appropriate for the sport. Parents should also evaluate whether inappropriate aggression is being reinforced in children, as this can affect a child's honesty, judgement, responsibility, trustworthiness, common sense, and a variety of other elements.

Families must control their TV sports viewing. In many households, television sporting events have become the centerpiece of holiday and weekend activities. If family time is spent watching a sports event, regard it in the same way as a live sporting event. Generally, tickets are only purchased for one live event. There may be many sports events in town, but fans must choose which event to attend. When many different sports are crammed into TV programming, choose one game to watch, just as you would only choose one live event to attend.

Controlling sports viewing may not be an easy task for many families. However, considering the unnecessary violence, the abundant commercials, and viewer expliotation, such a task would benefit parents and children alike.

18

Curbing Media Violence

"America—The Land of Opportunity," cried the early colonists as they set their feet upon the shores of this great land. To many, America still represents a land of opportunity. Though other nations have developed strongholds in areas formerly dominated by American industries, the United States is still the biggest and best in one particular area—entertainment.

We are purveyors of the most lucrative, sophisticated entertainment industry on earth. American made movies and television shows are popular world-wide. *Dallas, Moonlighting* and *The Cosby Show* can be seen in India, Japan, France and many other countries. The biggest box office hits in America are enjoyed by moviegoers the world over. One of the aftereffects of exporting popular American entertainment is that the rest of the world is made increasingly aware of the levels of violence that fill our media.

Today, has this land of opportunity become "The Land of Violence?" The truth is that from "sea to shining sea," Americans are more apt to commit violence than any other people of an industrialized nation on earth. In 1980, there were 8 reported handgun murders in England compared to 10,012 in the United States. During the past 50 years, our per capita rape rate has nearly increased 700 percent.[1] Over the past 30 years, our per capita homicide rate has almost doubled.[2] Between 1974 and 1983 the number of aggravated assaults has increased 6 percent, and child abuse by 48 percent.

Kids and Guns

Every evening pop-guns, squirt guns, cap-guns, bazookas, phasers, pistols, and machine guns are laid to rest in toy boxes and bedroom closets all over the United States until tomorrow's game of space combat, king-of-the-hill, or superheroes. It would be better if these toy guns stayed stashed away permanently. Guns are not fun, nor are they pleasant, wholesome or harmless. Toy guns provide a means for children to rehearse violent actions.

Statistics show that Americans don't need any more rehearsal with guns. Numbers of children die make-believe deaths in simulated battles and every day (in the real world) one child will be shot to death with a handgun.

Despite this grim figure, packing a real pistol has become a status symbol among school children. Students who carry guns are considered powerful by their peers. Many students who have no intention of using a gun to commit a crime argue that they must carry guns to protect themselves from class bullies who also bring guns to school. Fights that were formerly settled in hallways with arms swinging and fists flying now end in gunfire and blood.

Handguns in the Home

Three out of ten Americans keep guns in their homes for security reasons according to a 1987 Associated Press poll. Sales of handguns are up 10 percent over 1986. 58 percent of all purchases are for protection, though only 14 percent of handguns are actually used for protection. When asked why they buy handguns, most people say that they are driven by fear. Women buy handguns because they are afraid that they will encounter a rapist or burglar.

Guns that are purchased for security reasons actually make the home less secure. A gun in the home is 199 times more likely to kill a friend, family, or acquaintance than a criminal intruder.[3] So, where do many people get the idea that guns can protect them and keep their families secure?

Killing Made Too Easy

The use of violence in the media is perpetuating the notion that guns protect more than they harm and that violence is the best means to an end. Violence is glamorized in the media. Mugging, beating and killing are presented as thrilling action.

Since TV is the most pervading of all media, consider some of the leading characters from prime time drama, police, and adventure shows. Guns are the favorite weapons of TV's "good guys." They carry them constantly and rely on them to kill "bad" guys. Gun-toting heroes are themselves rarely if ever killed in gun fights. They receive only superficial wounds during their select prime-time position.

In both TV and movies, violence is depicted as the most successful and efficient way of resolving conflicts. The impersonal quality of killing in the media encourages viewers not to think of the victims as human beings. Instead, they entice us to think only of ourselves.

Romans 12:3: . . . *every man [ought] not to think of himself more highly than he ought to think* . . . .

Constant exposure to media violence hardens both children and adults to the reality of what a bullet can do. No matter what our natural disposition, watching on-screen violence gradually gnaws away at our ability to be sensitive, optimistic and kind to others.

Media's Best Interests Not Best For the Rest!

Ninety-eight percent of homes across the United States have at least one television. On the average, we watch more than six hours of TV a day. For the last 20 years, experts have studied how levels of on-screen violence affect levels of real-life violence. Many media executives keep protesting that there is no concrete proof to link media violence with growing levels of domestic violence. However, advertisers spend billions of dollars every year because they believe that TV *can* influence human behavior. Are network executives too busy crying, "No proof" to recognize the statement that is being made by the many advertisers filling their coffers [wallets]?

The mounting evidence does not sit well with the entertainment industry. Just as TV characters turn to violence as an easy way to solve frustration, so do programming executives. It is less expensive to do a shoot-out or a chase scene than it is to pay someone to write a segment of equal length that involves interaction and meaningful dialogue among three characters. **When confronted directly with the "epidemic" of media violence, most groups within the entertainment world want to lay blame on another group. Actors blame the writers and directors; directors blame producers; producers blame networks; and the networks blame the ratings system.**

Because of the current ratings system, the motivation of all TV networks can be expressed in one objective: to win the largest number of viewers during every half hour of every day. All other goals are secondary to that goal. If we assume that the ratings drive is the financial reality that underlies the problem of media violence, we can assume that the TV industry will always put corporate profits ahead of public interest. It can't afford to regulate itself or to offer public service programs. If one network gets ahead in the ratings, that translates into billions of dollars in advertising.

The media, acting in their own best interest, will continue to ignore the facts about on-screen violence. However, you now know the adverse effects of media violence on our society. You can no longer plead ignorance as an alibi for doing nothing. What do you want for your children? What kind of society do you wish to live in?

Truth or Consequences

You must ask yourself what it is you really want or be prepared to accept the consequences. Most parents can readily answer the question of what they want for their children by describing what they don't want. No mother hopes her child will grow to be an assassin or terrorist. No one ever wants to see his child serving a jail sentence for manslaughter or homicide.

The more difficult questions to answer include what kind of society do we want? What is our attitude about media violence? What are we prepared to do about media violence? Life in a free society affords many liberties to individuals and organizations. There will always be those who test the area of exercising their own freedoms while infringing on the rights of others.

In spite of their differences, most people living in a free society would agree that they want to live civilly, safely and peaceably. Consider that media violence encourages behaviors that threaten a civilized society.

What should be our individual attitude toward media violence? Why is it important to examine it? If we are confident that we are raising our children in a loving atmosphere, why shouldn't we be able to watch whatever programs we like?

What we *do* is important. **Jesus Christ challenged people's attitudes as much as he challenged their behavior. In His eyes, we are not only accountable for our own actions, we are also accountable for the effects those actions have on others.**

The last question you need to ask yourself is: what are you prepared to do about it? Individuals, parents, parent groups, school groups, churches and denominations of churches can do much to help curb media violence. The media is currently capitalizing on its right of free speech, guaranteed by the First Amendment. The rest of us also have the right to speak whatever we wish. Parents and concerned groups should take advantage of the means available in a free society to oppose the media's polluting of our minds and the minds of our children.

TV a Ticklish Tutor

The effects of TV violence can mold children's attitudes about aggression. The more TV that children watch, the more accepting they become about using hostility. Young viewers who watch a lot of TV are more likely to agree that if you are mad at someone, it is "almost always right" to be able to hit that person.

Too much TV watching makes people more suspicious of others and increases a person's belief that he will become a victim of real life violence. Heavy TV viewers begin to see the world as more dangerous than it actually is. They believe that other people aren't trustworthy and that other people would like to take advantage of them.

Because music video combines erotic material, teen idols, and violence, it requires careful monitoring. Existing research shows that MTV and its equivalents have a serious negative effect on children and teens.

A Less Hostile World

It is wishful thinking to believe that aggression can be eliminated in our society. However, there certainly are ways to reduce our aggression levels. Adults need to help children recognize that there is a link between behavior and its consequences. By using rewards and punishments, parents can teach children the effects of their actions.

Reward or Punishment Can Help Children Learn

Rewards and punishment can *reduce* or *increase* hostility and aggression. It depends on how they are used and to what extent. If parents punish aggressive acts and are not *overly* severe, they are more likely to raise nonviolent children. Rewards or punishment can be used to control violent tendencies in children. Here are our recommendations:

1. **Remove any reward a child gains through being aggressive.** For example, if a little boy takes a toy from his sister, mother should simply return the toy to her daughter, and the boy will no longer have the reward for his aggression.

2. **Reward cooperative behavior.** Unless the aggressive act is extremely severe and may result in someone being harmed, ignore it. An added bonus to this plan is that it encourages parents to express positive feelings to children.

3. **Expose children to persons who are kind and cooperative.** Children learn how to behave by watching adults. If parents want children to adopt cooperative behaviors, they should handle tough situations without becoming aggressive themselves. Set a good example for your children. At the same time, don't expose children to violent role models. If children want to watch an actor on TV who is violent, interest them in another program or turn off the TV and find another activity for them.

4. **Punish others who use violence. If children see someone being punished for their aggression, they are less likely to want to imitate that aggressive person.** Very small children, however, can only associate punishment with aggression if the punishment is immediate! If on TV a person robs a bank before the commercial, but goes to jail after the station break, small children cannot associate the crime with the punishment. They think a person can rob a bank and get away with it. We suggest that a responsible adult explain what is happening to the child.

5. **Create a peaceful environment.** Parents can designate play areas and encourage play to reduce conflicts among children. "The quality and quantity of children's play should not be taken lightly," *(Turmoil In The Toy Box)*.[4] Don't buy guns and other

239

weapons that encourage violent play. Toys and games that "stress or instill fear" in children should also be avoided.

6. **Teach Children To Care.** Children must be taught not only by word of mouth, but also by example to be sensitive to the feelings of victims. Those who can feel for victims are less likely to continue being aggressive toward others.

These recommendations are just a few ways we authors believe one can teach children to care.

Things Churches Can Do

For many churches, combating media violence begins with awareness. Church leaders should make their membership aware of the consequences of viewing media saturated with physical and sexual violence. On a very basic level, churches can become involved in curbing media violence by offering children and adults meaningful alternatives.

On the local level, church groups can encourage local TV stations and theaters to provide non-violent and constructive entertainment. (Programs about nature, travel, science and adventure are effective alternatives to violent movies and shows.) Churches should evaluate the content of video programming, and church-run schools should include classes to help children understand the message behind the media.

Cable TV is rapidly becoming America's standard delivery system. Due to the fact that cable TV is paid for by the viewer, its programming escapes federal regulation. Church groups can exert pressure on the area cable service to make lock box devices mandatory with every installation, resulting in more parental control.

On a broader level, churches can petition broadcast networks to use the rating system developed by the motion picture industry whenever they broadcast material. They can also request that a clear description be given when airing promotions for the show.

Churches can also appeal to the Federal Communications Commission (FCC) to abandon deregulation and resume its role as overseer of the air waves. As long as deregulation is in effect, networks will look toward physical and sexual violence as easy ways to keep audiences tuned in and ratings up. The entertainment industry is big business, but it is not like any other business. Television and videos come into the home, that makes them our responsibility.

Because peace is fundamental to the gospel, each "believer" must use whatever opportunities are available to emphasize non-violent ways to reduce conflicts between individuals, groups, and nations and to protest uncontrolled levels of violence in the media.

Things Parents Can Do

Parenting in these fast and somewhat permissive times can be challenging. Because so many families rely on two incomes, today's parents have more to do and less time to do it. Parents must accept the responsibility of supervising their children's TV viewing. Should we ask the government to assume responsibility for legislating what children watch on TV if parents are not willing to do it in their own home?

What are the reasons that parents allow their children to watch on-screen violence? Some parents are not aware of the effects of media violence. They may have heard that viewing media violence can increase levels of aggression, but don't see any behavior changes in their children. They, therefore, permit their children to watch what they want on TV, not realizing the adverse effects (layer upon layer) of media violence. Attempting to avoid an argument, other parents shrink from their responsibility. Could it be that these parents are TV addicts themselves and don't want to deal with the issue?

To help curb your child's exposure to media violence, we offer the following list of **Don'ts** and **Do's:**

DON'Ts

1. Don't buy violent toys for children.
2. Don't use TV as a punishment or reward.
3. Don't allow children unlimited viewing.
4. Don't go back on your word when you forbid them to watch a particular program.
5. Don't use the television, movies or videocassettes as a convenient baby-sitter.
6. Don't watch trash. If parents exercise bad judgement, how can they expect to influence a child's judgement for the better.
7. Don't put a TV in any room where the family meal is shared.
8. Don't merely tell children "Don't watch the TV."

DO's

1. Do set hourly limits on TV watching. Ten hours per week is more than enough.
2. Do watch children for mood swings, eyestrain and headaches —all symptoms of too much television.
3. Do turn off the TV set or VCR if there's any argument among children over a program.
4. Do keep a sharp eye on what children are watching. Decide in advance what programs will be watched in the home.
5. Do restrict young children from watching war,cartoons or those based on conflicts and fighting.
6. Do check that children show signs of having other interests. See what books they are reading and what projects they recently have completed.
7. Do watch TV and movies with your children and comment on what you see. Ask for their impressions if any material they see is questionable. Help children to understand each program's structure and values.

Should parents wish to become more involved, there are other things that can be done to influence public opinion on media violence. Consider some of these actions: Write letters to the editors of your local newspaper or to a magazine when you find any TV program, movie or videocassette objectionable. Write a letter to your Congressman. The Congress can enact legislation requiring the FCC to monitor network television, study violence, and publish the findings.

Parents' groups can be just as outspoken as church groups when writing to networks, cable TV companies, or the FCC. Parents can band together in groups of two dozen or more, refer to themselves as a coalition and organize themselves around a concern, such as mandatory lock boxes for cable subscribers. Parents can hold broadcasters to a higher level of responsibility. Network TV is directed by law to operate in the public interest. Though network TV is protected by the First Amendment right to free speech, parents need to demand more involvement on the part of the FCC. The FCC should be requiring networks to devote a percentage of air time and money to creative and constructive children's programming. The FCC should once again disallow program-length cartoons.

Parents can make their views known to the three major networks *(ABC, CBS, NBC)*, to the *FCC*, the *NCTV*, and to the *Motion Picture Association of America*.

(For your convenience, a list of names and addresses follows the Bibliography.)

Horror and Violence—
The Deadly Duo In The Media

Media violence is out of control! There is much we can do to stem the violent tide. By doing nothing, we are helping to perpetuate the media's message of violence. A society that values its freedom must encourage the mutual responsibility of every person for every other person, and for the welfare of the community. If parents, churches, and civic organizations are not willing to take responsibility for violence in the media, clearly no one will. The media is not going to self-impose restrictions on its own use of violence. We must act now. God has given us a commission like no other. We urge you to avoid the consequences of inaction. Ask yourself, "Am I willing to shoulder this awesome responsibility? Am I willing to slay these 'deadly' media giants?"

With God's help—YOU CAN!

Bibliography

CHAPTER ONE
1. Radecki, Thomas, MD, National Coalition On Television Violence Press Release, July 17, 1986.
2. *NCTV NEWS*, Volume 8, No. 7-8, Nov-Dec, 1987.
3. Radecki, Thomas, MD, National Coalition On Television Violence Press Release, No Date.

CHAPTER THREE
1. Broadman, Muriel, *Understanding Your Child's Entertainment*, Harper & Row, Publishers, New York, 1977, p. 132.
2. Leibert, Robert M., Joyce N. Sprafkin, and Emily S. Davidson, *The Early Window, Effects of Television On Children And Youth*, Pergamon Press, New York, 1982, p. 75.
3. Gitlin, Todd, *Inside Prime Time*, Pantheon Books, New York, 1983, p. 242.
4. Edgar, Patricia, *Children and Screen Violence*, 1979, p. 14.
5. Ibid, p. 29.

CHAPTER FOUR
1. Greenfield, Patricia Marks, *Mind And Media*, Harvard University Press, Cambridge, Massachusetts, 1984, p. 91.
2. Langone, John, *Violence! Our Fastest-Growing Public Health Problem*, Little, Brown and Company, Boston, 1984, pp. 50-51.
3. Faivelson, Saralie, "Verdict on TV Violence," *Woman's Day*, October 1, 1987, p. 24.
4. Langone, pp. 51-52.
5. Comstock, George, Steven Chaffee, Nathan Katzman, Maxwell McCombs, and Donald Roberts, *Television And Human Behavior*, Columbia University Press, New York, 1978, pp. 223-229.
6. Radecki, Thomas, MD, National Coalition On Television Violence Press Release, May 9, 1985.
7. Holahan, Jane, " 'Rambo III', Another Round of Ridiculous Violence," *New Era*, Lancaster, PA, May 26, 1988, p. 41.
8. Schwantes, Dave, *Taming Your TV And Other Media*, Southern Publishing Association, Nashville, Tennessee, pp. 80-81.
9. Mankiewicz, Frank and Joel Swerdlow, *Remote Control: Television And The Manipulation Of American Life*, Times Books, New York, 1978, p. 46.
10. Sanoff, Alvin P., "What is Hollywood Saying to us?" *U.S. News & World Report*, June 30, 1986, p.55.
11. Seuling, Barbara, *You Can't Show Kids In Underwear*, Doubleday & Company, New York, 1982, p. 8.
12. *NCTV NEWS*, Volume 6, Number 6-7, July-August 1985.
13. Radecki, Thomas, MD, NCTV Press Release, January 25, 1988.

CHAPTER FIVE

1. Schwantes, Dave, *Taming Your TV And Other Media*, Southern Publishing Association, Nashville, Tennessee, pp. 79-80.
2. Comstock, George, Steven Chaffee, Nathan Katzman, Maxwell McCombs, and Donald Roberts, *Television And Human Behavior*, Columbia University Press, New York, 1978, pp. 223-231.
3. Huesmann, L. Rowell and Leonard D. Eron, *Television And The Aggressive Child: A Cross-National Comparison*, Lawrence Erlbaum Associates, Publishers, Hillsdale, New Jersey, 1986, p. 10.
4. Ibid, p. 15.
5. Mankiewicz, Frank and Joel Swerdlow, *Remote Control*, Times Books, New York, 1978, p. 53.
6. Moody, Kate, *Growing Up On Television*, Times Books, New York, 1984, p. 81-85.

CHAPTER SIX

1. Wilkins, Joan Anderson, *Breaking The TV Habit*, Charles Scribner's Sons, New York, pp. 37-38, 65-66.
2. Faivelson, Saralie, "Verdict On TV Violence," *Woman's Day*, October 1, 1987, p. 24.
3. Wilkins, p. 32.
4. Palmer, Edward L. and Aimee Dorr, *Children And The Faces Of Television*, Academic Press, New York, 1980, pp. 157-159.
5. Radecki, Thomas, MD, Editor, "Adolescents' Fright Reactions," *NCTV NEWS*, Volume 3, No. 2-3, March-May 1982, p. 3.
6. Stein, Ben, *The View From Sunset Boulevard*, Basic Books, Inc., New York, pp. 40-46.
7. Schwantes, Dave, *Taming Your TV And Other Media*, Southern Publishing Association, Nashville, Tennessee, p. 82.

CHAPTER SEVEN

1. Statistical Abstracts Of The United States, "Law Enforcement, Courts, and Prisons, Crime Rates," 1986.
2. Langone, John, *Violence! Our Fastest-Growing Public Health Problem*, Little, Brown and Company, Boston, 1984, p. 51.
3. Ibid, pp. 48-49.
4. Wilkins, Joan Anderson, *Breaking The TV Habit*, Charles Scribner's Sons, New York, p. 11.
5. Winn, Marie, *The Plug-In Drug*, Viking, New York, 1985, p. 101.
6. Radecki, Thomas, MD, National Coalition On Television Violence Press Release, December 30, 1987.

CHAPTER EIGHT

1. Wilkins, Joan Anderson, *Breaking The TV Habit*, Charles Scribner's Sons, New York, 1983, pp. 6-7.
2. Ibid, p.16.
3. Ibid, p. 17.
4. Schwantes, Dave, *Taming Your TV And Other Media*, Southern Publishing Association, Nashville, Tennessee, pp. 72-73.

5. Schwantes, pp. 74-75.
6. Broadman, Muriel, *Understanding Your Child's Entertainment*, Harper & Row, Publishers, New York 1977, p. 144-145.
7. Liebert, Robert M., Joyce N. Sprafkin, and Emily S. Davidson, *The Early Window, Effects Of Television On Children And Youth*, Pergamon Press, New York, 1983, pp. 131-133.

CHAPTER NINE

1. Schwantes, Dave, *Taming Your TV And Other Media*, Southern Publishing Association, Nashville, Tennessee, p. 74-75.
2. Langone, John, *Violence! Our Fastest-Growing Public Health Problem*, Little, Brown and Company, Boston, 1984, pp. 49-50.
3. Liebert, Robert M., Joyce N. Sprafkin, and Emily S. Davidson, *The Early Window, Effects Of Television On Children And Youth*, Pergamon Press, New York, p. 50.
4. Ibid, pp. 51-52.
5. Ibid, pp. 58-59.
6. Comstock, George, Steven Chaffee, Nathan Katzman, Maxwell McCombs, and Donald Roberts, *Television And Human Behavior*, Columbia University Press, New York, 1978, pp. 229-231.
7. Schwantes, pp. 77-79.
8. Huesmann, L. Rowell and Leonard D. Eron, *Television And The Aggressive Child: A Cross-National Comparison*, Lawrence Erlbaum Associates, Publishers, New Jersey, 1986, P. 239.
9. Ibid, P. 7.
10. Ibid, P. 32.

CHAPTER TEN

1. Seuling, Barbara, *You Can't Show Kids In Underwear And Other Little-Known Facts About Television*, Doubleday, New York, 1982, p. 82.
2. Moody, Kate, *Growing Up On Television*, Times Books, New York, 1980, p. 94.
3. Liebert, Robert M., Joyce N. Sprafkin, and Emily S. Davidson, *The Early Window, Effects Of Television On Children And Youth*, Pergamon Press, New York, 1982, p. 148.
4. Ibid, pp. 148-149.
5. Gitlin, Todd, *Inside Prime Time*, Pantheon Books, New York, 1983, pp. 93-94.
6. "NCTV Briefs," *NCTV NEWS*, Volume 9, Number 1-2, Jan.-Feb., 1988, p. 12.
7. Ibid, p. 2.
8. *NCTV NEWS*, Volume 6, Number 3-4, Mar.-Apr., 1985, p. 7.
9. "Coke Uses Violence To Sell Soft Drink," *NCTV NEWS*, Volume 9, Number 1-2, Jan.-Feb., 1988, p. 11.
10. Barnouw, Erik, *Tube Of Plenty*, Oxford University Press, New York, 1975, pp. 132-133.
11. Mankiewicz, Frank and Joel Swerdlow, *Remote Control*, Times Books, New York, 1978, pp. 232-233.
12. "TV Distorts, says Meredith Baxter Birney," *Sunday News*, Lancaster, PA, Mar. 27, 1988, p. E3.

CHAPTER ELEVEN

1. "Toy and Play Violence," *NCTV NEWS*, Vol. 4, No. 4, July-August 1983, p. 12.
2. "Toy Companies Unwisely Promote War To Children," *NCTV NEWS*, Vol. 6, No. 6-7, July-August, 1985, p. 1.
3. Frame, Randy, "Violence For Fun," *Christianity Today*, Feb. 21, 1986, p. 16.
4. "New England War Registers League Newsletter," p. 1.
5. Englehardt, *Watching Television*, p. 77.
6. NCTV Press Release, Nov. 27, 1987, p. 2
7. Ibid.
8. NCTV Press Release, Jan. 15, 1987, p. 2.

CHAPTER TWELVE

1. Schwantes, Dave, *Taming Your TV And Other Media*, Southern Publishing Association, Nashville, Tennessee, p. 51.
2. Mankiewicz, Frank and Joel Swerdlow, *Remote Control*, Times Books, New York, 1978, p. 28.
3. Ibid, p. 28.
4. Ibid, p. 28.
5. Spock, Benjamin, MD, "How on-screen violence hurts your kids," *REDBOOK*, November, 1987, p. 26.
6. Wilkins, Joan Anderson, *Breaking The TV Habit*, Charles Scribner's Sons, New York, 1983, pp. 33-34.
7. Enos, Sondra Forsythe, "Living In Truly Tasteless Times," *Ladies' Home Journal*, November 1987, pp. 130, 184.
8. Winn, Marie, *The Plug-In Drug*, Viking, New York, 1977, pp. 105-106.
9. Mankiewicz, p. 39
10. "Surgeon General Says TV Immunizes Us To Violence," *NCTV NEWS*, Volume 5, No. 5-6, May-June 1984, p. 1.
11. "Woman Raped At McCaskey," *Intelligencer Journal*, Lancaster, PA, No. 255, April 11, 1988, p. 34.
12. Mander, Jerry, *Four Arguments For The Elimination Of Television*, William Morrow and Company, Inc., New York, 1978, p. 236.
13. Mankiewicz, p. 29.
14. Ibid, p. 34.
15. Broadman, Muriel, *Understanding Your Child's Entertainment*, Harper & Row, Publishers, New York, 1977, pp. 130-131.

CHAPTER THIRTEEN

1. Schwantes, Dave, *Taming Your TV And Other Media*, Southern Publishing Association, Nashville, Tennessee, p. 80.
2. Radecki, Thomas, MD, National Coalition on Television Violence Press Release, January 15, 1987.
3. "NCTV Cheers Alex Karras & TV GUIDE," *NCTV NEWS*, Volume 6, No. 9-10, September-December 1985, p. 10.
4. Radecki, Thomas, MD, Press Release, National Coalition on Television Violence, December 30, 1987.
5. Radecki, January 15, 1987.

BIBLIOGRAPHY

6. Frame, Randy, "Violence For Fun," *Christianity Today*, February 21, 1986, p. 16.

7. Fore, William F., "Media Violence: Hazardous To Our Health," *The Christian Century*, September 25, 1985, p. 834.

8. Hackett, George with Richard Sandea, Frank Gibney, Jr., and Robin Gareiss, "Kids: Deadly Force," *Newsweek*, January 11, 1988, p. 19.

9. Winn, Marie, *The Plug-In Drug*, Viking, New York, 1985, p. 108.

10. Radecki, Thomas, MD, Hearings on "Social Behavioral Effects of Violence Television," U.S. House of Representatives Subcommittee on Telecommunications, Consumer Protection and Finance, October 21, 1981.

11. Winn, p. 99.

12. Leibert, Robert M., Joyce Sprafkin, and Emily S. Davidson, *The Early Window, Effects Of Television On Children And Youth*, Pergamon Press, New York, 1983, p. 117.

13. Ibid, pp. 133-135.

14. Mankiewicz, pp. 15-17.

15. Karlen, Neal with Michael Reese, "A Copycat Assault?" *Newsweek*, October 22, 1984, p. 38.

16. Schwantes, pp. 80-81.

17. *NCTV NEWS*, October 8, 1980.

CHAPTER FOURTEEN

1. Malamuth, Neil, "Media's New Mood: Sexual Violence," *Media & Values*, Number 33, Fall 1985, p. 4.

2. Flander, Judy, "Television Targets Women As Victims," *Media & Values*, Number 33, Fall 1985, p. 12.

3. Ibid, p. 13.

4. "Alcohol and Drugs Flow Freely in Hollywood Films, *NCTV NEWS*, Volume 8, No. 7-8, Nov-Dec, 1987, p. 8.

5. "Teens: Rape Sometimes OK," *Intelligencer Journal*, Lancaster, PA, No. 274, May 3, 1988.

6. Malamuth, pp. 3-4.

7. "Junior Leagues Work on Videocassette Legislation," *NCTV NEWS*, Volume 8, No. 3-4, July-August, 1987, p. 1.

8. Martin, Mick and Marsha Porter, *Video Movie Guide 1988*, Ballantine Books, New York, 1987, pp. 838, 846, 849.

9. Frame, Randy, "Violence For Fun," *Christianity Today*, February 21, 1986, p. 16.

10. Anonymous, "Video Seduction," *Moody Monthly*, May 1987, pp. 28-30.

CHAPTER FIFTEEN

1. Radecki, Thomas, MD, International Coalition Against Violent Entertainment Press Release, April 20, 1987.

2. McGuigan, Cathleen with Janet Huck, "What Makes Arnold Run?" *Newsweek*, December 7, 1987, pp. 84-86.

3. "Christian Children's Book Makes Revision After NCTV Points Out Error," *NCTV NEWS*, Volume 7, No. 1-2, Jan-Mar, 1986, p. 6.

4. "Clint Eastwood Movie Causes Shooting," *NCTV NEWS*, Volume 4, No. 5-6, Sept-Oct 1983, p. 6.

5. "20, 21, & 22nd Deerhunter Shootings & Others," *NCTV NEWS*, Volume 2, No. 4, Jul-Aug 1981, p. 3.

CHAPTER SIXTEEN

1. Powell, Stewart, et al., "What Entertainers are Doing to Your Kids," *U.S. NEWS & WORLD REPORT*, October 28, 1985, p. 46.
2. Enos, Sondra Forsythe, "Truly Tastless Times," *Ladies' Home Journal*, November 1984, p. 48.
3. Ibid.
4. "Rock Music Violence Update," *NCTV NEWS*, Vol. 6, No. 9-10, Sept-Dec 1985, p. 10.
5. Gore, Tipper, *Raising PG Kids In An X-Rated Society*, Abingdon Press, Nashville, 1987, p. 120.
6. Ibid, p. 58.
7. *NCTV MUSICVIDEO REPORT*, P. 1.
8. "Still No Videogame Violence Research," *NCTV NEWS*, Vol. 4. No. 1, Oct. 1982-Jan. 1983, p. 5.
9. "One Million Sold In One Day," *COMPUTE!*, Volume 10, No. 6 Issue 97, June 1988, p. 7.
10. Greenfield, Patricia Marks, *Mind And Media*, Harvard University Press, Cambridge, Massachusetts, 1984, p. 102.
11. *NCTV NEWS*, Vol. 4, No. 5-6, Sept-Oct 1983.
12. "Children and Video: Computing The Effects," *Consumer's Research Magazine*, Vol. 69, June 1986, p. 20.
13. "Videogame Review," *NCTV NEWS*, Vol. 4, No 1, Oct 1982-Jan 1983, p.11.
14. Wilkins, Joan Anderson, *Breaking The TV Habit*, Charles Scribner's Sons, New York, 1982, p. 124.
15. "Videogame Review," p. 11.

CHAPTER SEVENTEEN

1. "TV Sports Violence: A Serious Problem," *NCTV NEWS*. Vol. 5, No. 1-2, Jan-Feb 1984, p. 3.
2. "Los Angeles Raiders: Dirty Image," *NCTV NEWS*, Vol. 5, No. 1-2, Jan-Feb 1984, p. 1.
3. Koppett, Leonard, *Sports Illusion, Sports Reality: A Reporter's View Of Sports Journalism And Society*, Houghton Mifflin Company, Boston, 1981, pp. 120-121.
4. "Televised Sports and Aggression," *NCTV NEWS*, Vol. 2, No. 3, April 1981, p. 6.
5. "More Research on Boxing," *NCTV NEWS*, Vol 7, No. 5-6, June-July 1986, p. 4. Lundberg, George D., Journal Of The American Medical Association, Vol. 255, No. 18, May 9, 1986, p. 2484.
6. "NCTV Protests Violence of Professional Wrestling," *NCTV NEWS*, Vol. 6, No. 3, March-April 1985, p. 3.
7. Koppett, p. 215.
8. "Winning is Everything," *NCTV NEWS*, Vol. 5, No. 1-2, Jan-Feb 1984, p. 2.
9. Cosell, *I Never Played The Game*, William Morrow and Co., New York, 1985, p. 5.

CHAPTER EIGHTEEN

1. Policy Statement, National Council of The Churches of Christ in the U.S.A. Communication Commission, Nov. 6, 1986, p. 2.
2. Fore, William F., "Media Violence Hazardous To Our Health," *The Christian Century*, Spetember 25, 1985, p. 834.
3. "Owning A Gun Doesn't Increase A Secure Feeling," *NCTV NEWS*, Vol. 8. No. 7-8, Nov-Dec 1987, p. 5.
4. Phillips, Phil, *Turmoil In The Toy Box*, Starburst Publishers, Lancaster, Pennsylvania, 1986, p. 28.

ABC-TV
1330 Avenue of the Americas
New York, New York 10019

CBS Entertainment
51 W. 52nd Street
New York, NY 10019

NBC-TV
30 Rockefeller Plaza
New York, NY 10020

American Family Association
Donald E. Wildmon
Post Office Drawer 2440
Tupelo, Mississippi 38803

Motion Picture Association of America
1133 Avenue of the Americas
New York, NY 10036

National Coalition on Television Violence
Dr. Thomas Radecki, M.D.
P.O. Box 2157
Champaign, IL 61820

Federal Communications Commission
1919 M Street NW
Washington, D.C. 20554

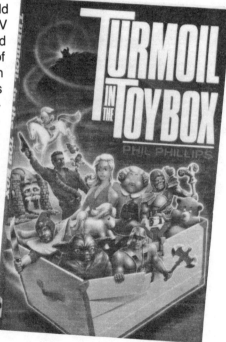

Books & Tapes on Related Topics

Turmoil In The Toy Box—video   —Phil Phillips

This eye-opening video, featuring Phil Phillips and host Gary Greenwald, takes an indepth look at the rise of the occult and pagan religions within the toy and cartoon industries. Contains actual examples of toys and film clips from popular TV cartoons.

(90 min. tape—VHS only) 0006563589 **$34.95**

Turmoil In The Toy Box II—audio   —Joan Hake Robie

Narrated by Joan Hake Robie, author of the book *Turmoil In The Toy Box II,* this 60 minute audio explains how many parents don't realize the role that toys and cartoons play in their child's life. It reveals some of the hidden and not so hidden messages directed to the minds of our children.

(audio cassette tape) 0914984268   **$7.95**

The Truth About Dungeons And Dragons—audio

—Joan Hake Robie

Explains the game of Dungeons and Dragons and lists the bizarre cast of characters which includes demons, dragons, witches, zombies, harpies, gnomes and creatures who cast spells and exercise supernatural powers. It tells how Dungeons and Dragons dabbles in the occult, encourages sex and violence and is a form of Devil worship.

(audio cassette tape) 091498425X   **$7.95**

The Great Pretender   —Rose Hall Warnke & Joan Hake Robie

An amusing, revealing, and oftimes shocking look into the life and ministry of Mike and Rose Warnke—uncovers the suspense, danger, joy and sorrow that surrounds a ministry that declares war on Satan.

(trade paper) ISBN 0914984039   **$8.95**

Courting The King Of Terrors

—Frank Carl with Joan Hake Robie

This book probes the relentless ills that are destroying the American family, and offers counsel to families in crisis. Learn the warning signals of suicide and other self-destructive behavior. "I know about suicide," says Frank Carl. "I lost a Brother and a Sister to that monster!"

(trade paper) ISBN 0914984187   **$7.95**

The Rock Report   —Fletcher A. Brothers

An "uncensored" look into today's Rock Music scene—provides the reader with the necessary information and illustrations to make intelligent decisions about rock music and its influence on the mind.

(trade paper) ISBN 0914984136   **$6.95**

Other Books by Starburst Publishers

Reverse The Curse In Your Life — Joan Hake Robie
(trade paper) ISBN 0914984241 **$6.95**

The Quest For Truth — Ken Johnson
(trade paper) ISBN 0914984217 **$7.95**

Man And Wife For Life — Joseph Kanzlemar, Ed.D.
(trade paper) ISBN 0914984233 **$7.95**

A Candle In Darkness (novel) — June Livesay
(trade paper) ISBN 0914984225 **$8.95**

Alzheimer's—Does "The System Care?"
—.Ted Valenti, M.S.W. & Paula Valenti, R.N.
(hard cover) 0914984179 **$14.95**

The Subtle Snare — Joan Hake Robie
(trade paper) ISBN 0914984128 **$8.95**

Inch by Inch . . . Is It a Cinch? — Phyllis Miller
(trade paper) ISBN 0914984152 **$8.95**

Devotion in Motion — Joan Hake Robie
(trade paper) ISBN 0914984004 **$4.95**

You Can Live In Divine Health — Joyce Boisseau
(trade paper) ISBN 0914984020 **$6.95**

To My Jewish Friends With Love — Christine Hyle
(booklet) 0006028098 **$1.00**

Purchasing Information

Most listed books and tapes are available from your favorite Bookstore, either from current stock or special order. You may also order direct from STARBURST PUBLISHERS. When ordering enclose full payment plus $1.50* for shipping and handling ($2.50* if Canada or Overseas). Payment in US Funds only. Please allow three to four weeks for delivery. Make checks payable to and mail to STARBURST PUBLISHERS, P.O. Box 4123, LANCASTER, PA 17604. Prices subject to change without notice. Catalog available upon request.

* We reserve the right to ship your order the least expensive way. If you desire first class (domestic) or air shipment (overseas) please enclose additional funds as follows: First Class within the USA and Canada enclose $2.00. Airmail Overseas enclose 30% of total order. These amounts are in addition to the base shipping costs listed in the previous paragragh. All remittance must be in US Funds.